Healthy Breaks

The first complete guide
to health farms, hotels, spas
and centres in the British Isles

Catherine Beattie

Discovery Books

Published in association with the National Tourist Boards
of England, Wales, Scotland and Northern Ireland

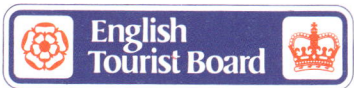  

© Catherine Beattie 1992

Discovery Books
29 Hacketts Lane, Pyrford, Woking, Surrey GU22 8PP

Typesetting and design by
Tim Harland, Hyden House Limited, Clanfield, Hampshire

Symbols
Paul Butler

Printed by
Craft Print

British Library Cataloguing in Publication Data
A catalogue record for this book is available from the British Library.

ISBN 0 9518511 0 1

All rights reserved. No part of this publication may be reproduced, stored in a retrieval system, rebound or transmitted in any form or by any means, electronic, mechanical, photocopying, recording or otherwise, without the prior written permission of Discovery Books.

The contents of this publication are believed correct at the time of printing. However, the publishers and the National Tourist Boards of England, Wales, Scotland and Northern Ireland cannot accept responsibility for errors or omissions, nor for changes in policy or details given. We have tried to ensure accuracy in this guide, but readers should always satisfy themselves that the facilities they require are available and that prices, where quoted, still apply.

Cover pictures: Sopwell House Hotel & Country Club (see page 77)

CONTENTS

Foreword	5
Introduction to:	
Health Farms & Hydros	7
Hotels	11
Family Resorts	13
Price Categories	14
Symbol Key	15
Directory of Establishments:	
Southern England	17
South West England	89
Central England	113
Northern England	151
Wales	189
Scotland	199
Ireland	225
British Spas	240
Glossary of Treatments & Therapies	249

ACKNOWLEDGEMENTS

I should like to acknowledge those who have helped me in the writing and publication of this book.

My warmest thanks to Richard Thomas for his enthusiasm, unwavering support and practical help at all times; to Tim Harland for designing and typesetting the manuscript and to the English Tourist Board for help and advice. I should also like to record my appreciation of the generous hospitality and assistance given by health farms, resorts and hotels.

Finally, special thanks to my husband, Alec for keeping the home fires burning and encouraging me throughout, and to my children, Julie, Clare, Kevin, Sarah, Alison, Jonathan, Thomas and Stephen, who put up with the many hours I spent glued to my word processor, with only an occasional moan.

FOREWORD

I decided to write this book when I worked on a health magazine and could never find a publication about health farms to recommend to the many readers asking for one. Excellent guides were readily available on every other type of holiday, but nothing specifically about health farms and what they offered in the way of treatments and facilities. I have therefore included details of *every* health farm I found to be currently operating in the British Isles - from the famous Champneys to the simplistic Lios Dana in rural Ireland. I make no claim that the list is either selective or exhaustive - new establishments are probably opening up as I write this!

To give as comprehensive a choice of healthy break as possible, details of spas, resorts and a selection of hotels offering leisure and treatment facilities are also included. After all, not everyone wants the dietary restrictions of a health farm or separation from their children (no under 16s at health farms) when taking a short holiday.

The criterion for inclusion in *Healthy Breaks* is that all establishments offer a residential stay combined with optional body, beauty or health treatments, with suggestions ranging from the most homely and inexpensive to the ultimate in luxurious pampering. Reasonably priced health farms in Northern Ireland and the Irish Republic have also been included. They offer an unusual and different type of healthy break, worth considering if a complete change of environment and pace of life is desired.

Writing and researching the guide was challenging and time consuming. I visited many establishments, trying out treatments, exercise classes, food and facilities, and chatted to owners, managers, therapists and guests. Unfortunately, time did not allow me to visit *every* entry, so my research includes information compiled from family members, friends and colleagues. I sent out detailed questionnaires and letters, and made numerous phone calls to ensure all particulars were as accurate and up-to-date as possible. As changes of policy and ownership do occur from time to time, always obtain confirmation of current prices and amenities before making a firm reservation. All establishments in this guide will be delighted to send brochures and current prices on request (please mention reading about them in *Healthy Breaks*). If you intend having extra treatments, it is a good idea to book these when reserving accommodation, as some popular ones get booked up surprisingly quickly.

I hope you will enjoy reading *Healthy Breaks* and that it will prove a useful and informative guide. Please send me your comments - I would be especially interested to hear of any other health farms, resorts or hotels that could be included in a second edition.

Catherine Beattie
January 1992

INTRODUCTION TO HEALTHY BREAKS

Champneys at Gleneagles

There has never been a better time to enjoy a healthy holiday break. Health farms, spas, resorts and hotels are all catering for increasing numbers of people seeking a few days' relaxation and pampering. Customer choice is improving all the time, as new establishments open and existing ones upgrade accommodation and facilities.

Health farm, resort or hotel - how do they compare for atmosphere, facilities and value for money?

Health Farms & Hydros

British health farms have come a long way from the clinically austere 'fat farms' of the 50s and 60s, when fasting and cold showers were an integral part of a regime geared mainly to weight loss for the rich and famous. The spartan image has been replaced by cheerful informality, echoed in homely comforts like carpeted floors and relaxing lounges adorned with restful green foliage. Modern health farms are for *everyone,* offering a nurtured environment in which to enjoy a few days' self indulgence, whilst being pampered with relaxing treatments, healthy food and a wealth of exercise opportunities.

The majority of health farms are not as grandiose as their enticing brochures and glamorous media image portray. Often based in historic manor houses amid acres of beautiful grounds, the ambience is friendly and comfortable rather than ritzy. Many visitors come by themselves and the friendly atmosphere is conducive to making new friends, even on the shortest break.

What To Take
Packing for a healthy break is surprisingly easy as ordinary day clothes can be left at home. The only essentials to remember are swimwear, leisure or track suit, flip-flops, trainers and exercise gear - and of course the ubiquitous towelling bathrobe which can be worn throughout the day. Bring a change of clothes if you like to dress for dinner and personal toiletries like shower gel, shampoo and conditioner, for these are not always supplied. Clothing and other items can usually be purchased from the 'in house' boutique, should you forget your socks or desire something new.

Food & Drink
Meals consist of a light breakfast often served in your room at around 7.30 am, a soup and salad lunch and a hot evening meal. Vegetarian options are always available, as well as plentiful supplies of filler foods like bread rolls and jacket potatoes. There are no chocolate biscuits or fattening snacks of course, but tasty low calorie cake is sometimes served with afternoon tea.

All establishments serve 'healthy' dishes, some more imaginatively than others, but only those on a strict diet should feel the odd hunger pang. Dieters are well catered for with calorie counted menus and an abundance of salads, fresh vegetables and fruit. Special areas serving diet meals are often set aside for slimmers who can graduate to the main dining room and more substantial menus once they have achieved the desired weight loss. Given advanced notice, most health farm chefs can accommodate the needs of guests on special diets - diabetic, gluten-free, etc.

Fasting is rarely encouraged; weight loss is achieved through exercise and healthy eating. The simple formula of personally prescribed treatments, exercise and low calorie menus is an effective combination for ridding mind and body of stress, tension and surplus poundage!

Some health farms have a relaxed attitude to serving wine with meals, among them Ragdale Hall, Stobo Castle and Hoar Cross Hall. One half bottle per guest is the daily ration at Champneys, and can be taken with lunch or dinner or shared between the two meals. By contrast, alcohol is strictly taboo at many other establishments including Roundelwood, Forest Mere and Grayshott Hall.

Everyone is encouraged to help themselves to free (as a rule) non-alcoholic drinks (tea, coffee, soft drinks, etc) throughout the day, as it is important to replace body fluids lost during heat treatments and exercise. Some serious health establishments serve only herb teas and mineral water, regular tea and coffee is not available.

Treatments
After checking in at Reception, you are shown your room and taken around the facilities. After this comes the personal consultation with the doctor, nursing sister or therapist so a timetable of treatments can be scheduled. Some consultations are only cursory checks of weight and blood pressure while others take a full medical history before considering treatments and individual diet choices.

All health farms have some 'free' treatments included in the basic cost of a visit, the actual number depending on the length of stay. The daily rate commonly covers accommodation, meals, one heat treatment (sauna or steam) and one body massage per day. The tariff also includes all exercise classes, evening talks, demonstrations and use of sports facilities including the swimming pool. Always check exactly what treatments are included, especially if you plan a weekend stay. Sunday treatments are not available at all health farms, so weekend visitors have to fit them in on Fridays and Saturdays - all other facilities are available seven days a week.

If you like more than one heat treatment daily, ask if these can be taken without restriction. Progressive health farms allow free access to these 'wet' amenities, appreciating that visitors enjoy using the steam room or sauna when taking an early morning dip or late evening swim.

Because inclusive treatments are limited (there are some exceptions like Tyringham and Roundelwood with generous allocations), it is tempting to try out the extensive optional range on offer. Be aware that indulging in several of these hedonistic treats will add considerably to your final bill. Budget for one or two special treats like aromatherapy - expensive, but wonderfully self-indulgent and relaxing, a heated body wrap for sheer enjoyment and instant (temporary) loss of inches, or maybe a facial, manicure or pedicure to lift the spirits and boost morale.

Certain treatments such as aromatherapy, steam and sauna are not advised for pregnant women or those with high blood pressure. Others cannot be combined safely; a sunbed is not good for the skin after a deep facial like Cathiodermie, and fainting can be the result of taking a steam bath too soon after a soporific treatment like aromatherapy. Always ask a member of staff if you are unsure about the suitability of specific treatments.

Leisure & Sport
Sporting and exercise amenities vary greatly from one establishment to another. Organised walks and jogging are the most popular outdoor pursuits and there are often tennis courts and bicycles for hire. Tennis (and bridge) enthusiasts can advertise for partners on the noticeboard. Some health farms have an outdoor swimming pool or the advantage of a golf course which is always a bonus for keen players.

Exercise classes cover all types of activity, from gentle body toning and yoga to vigorous aerobics. Visitors used to regular work-outs are sometimes disappointed that the routines are not punishing enough.

Most health farms have a gymnasium of sorts, with instruction available on the safe use of the apparatus. Beginners should only use equipment when supervised. Fitness assessment programmes are becoming a popular option at many establishments, with individual exercise schedules drawn up for continuation at home. Occasionally the gymnasium has to double as an exercise studio, which can be irritating if you want to use the apparatus when the aerobics class is in full swing.

Accommodation
Bedrooms in most health farms are well decorated with comfortable beds and television. However standards of comfort do vary, even within the same establishment, with luxury accommodation at one end of the price scale and basic lower priced rooms at the other. Many of these 'budget' rooms are small, without a good view and have shared bathroom facilities. If you can afford the higher cost, opt for a room with a bathroom. Enjoyment of treatments, swimming, aerobics classes, etc, is enhanced by having your own clutter to return to between the various activities, where you can shower, change your clothes or wash your hair in peace.

Other General Information
There is no point in lazing in bed til noon at a health farm if you want to get the most out of your stay. The routine is firmly geared to an 'early to bed, early to rise' pattern, with the first activities of the day starting around 7.00 am. Time passes quickly with treatments, classes and sporting activities. By comparison, the quiet hours after the evening meal (taken relatively early) can seem tedious. To counteract boredom and encourage residents to mix socially, talks and discussion groups are held on topics as varied as alternative health, flower arranging, stress management, beauty and personal relationships. Evening outings to local places of interest are also arranged - but **not** visits to the nearest pub or fish and chip shop!

Health farms do not allow smoking in public areas and some have non-smoking bedrooms. Smokers are provided with their own lounge where a last cigarette and some animated late night chat are frequently enjoyed after most residents have departed to an early bed.

Despite a recession, health farms are currently enjoying a boom in popularity with people of all ages from all walks of life - weary mums, secretaries, teachers, nurses, business executives, show biz personalities and royalty. Health farms are still used by more women than men, although male numbers are slowly increasing, thanks to special fitness and de-stress programmes designed for them. Health farms do not accommodate children under the age of 16 years - the restful atmosphere and unsupervised recreational areas are not safe or suitable for them.

It has never been easy deciding which health farm to visit and whether it offers good value for money, which is one of the reasons this book was written. Until *Healthy Breaks* was published, not even a comprehensive list of health farms was available, far less an official association to monitor standards of accommodation, treatments and facilities. No rating system currently exists for health farms like that of the well recognised crowns awarded to hotels by the National Tourist Boards. Future editions of *Healthy Breaks* intend changing this state of affairs by either devising our own rating system or persuading health farms to form a register or association, so watch this space!

Hotels With Leisure & Treatment Facilities

British hotels have undergone a complete transformation over the last decade or so, with ever-improving standards of accommodation, food and amenities. Bargain weekend rates and provision of leisure facilities have tempted many visitors to try a short break for the first time.

Health and fitness is big business in the industry with all new hotel design incorporating leisure facilities whenever possible. Luxury hotels like Chewton Glen and Turnberry have had millions invested in superb new spa and leisure clubs offering the highest standards of comfort and luxury. Even relatively modest hotels often have outstanding health clubs and low priced weekend packages, ideal for families wanting a short break.

The British Isles has a wealth of wonderful country house hotels and many owners have now invested in leisure, as costs can be offset by running the leisure amenities as a separate entity in the form of an exclusive country club. Membership is limited to avoid overcrowding the facilities which are available to all hotel residents during their stay.

Many leisure and sporting amenities are entirely free, and others like squash and solaria, have nominal charges. Body and beauty treatments are paid for as taken, except when included as part of special health and fitness packages. Leisure clubs are run on similar lines to health farms, but even the most luxurious hotel cannot create the comfortable ambience of the health farm, where relaxation and rejuvenation are the sole purpose of a stay, and where you can walk around all day and eat meals in your bathrobe if you so wish!

Sports facilities such as tennis, squash, multi-station gymnasia and golf are utilised by the business visitor during the week and the leisure guest at weekends. Hotel leisure clubs remain open until late and access to spa pools, sauna and steam rooms is unlimited and free - a more generous use of facilities than many health farms who allow only one heat treatment a day and charge if you want an extra one.

Hotels do not offer discussion groups, demonstrations or make-up classes in the evening, of course; these are the prerogative of the health farm. However, exercise and aerobic classes are often of a higher standard, thanks to the fitness of the club members who regularly attend them. In the gymnasium, a more varied selection of high quality equipment is usually available offering a better choice and standard than at the average health farm.

Body and beauty therapies are much the same wherever you are lucky enough to enjoy them! Some establishments may have their own special treatments in addition those available everywhere like G5 massage and Slendertone. Beauticians and therapists have similar qualifications and training wherever they work, and manufacturers of the most popular products used in salons provide full training in the specialised application of their products.

Hotels have a livelier atmosphere than health farms which are naturally more quiet and restful and never hold Saturday night dinner dances! Bedrooms are generally of a good or excellent standard and invariably have an en suite bathroom. Children are welcome and accommodated free when sharing with parents, or at discounted rates when occupying their own room, with special meals, baby-sitting and creche facilities often provided.

One of the pleasures of staying at an hotel is of course the food. Enormous breakfasts, appetising lunches and memorable dinners are great when you are not watching your weight. Slimmers able to resist such temptations, have lots of choice too, as low fat vegetarian dishes, fresh fruit, vegetables and salads are always on the menu.

Many spa and seaside towns have palatial hotels built in Victorian or Edwardian times, now fully refurbished and renovated to a high standard. The excellent facilities of these quality hotels enable the visitor to enjoy a holiday to the full - even in unpredictable British weather. A stay at one of these premier hotels is not inexpensive, but compares quite favourably with health farm charges, from about £130 per person for two nights' accommodation, dinner, bed and breakfast and full use of health and leisure facilities.

Family Resorts

All-season family resorts, or 'holiday villages' as they are sometimes called, are relatively new to Britain and provide an opportunity for the whole family to enjoy a healthy break together, even in inclement weather.

The resorts are completely self-contained complexes, with shops, restaurants, cafes, bars and entertainments provided on site. Sports and leisure facilities are excellent indoors and out, with sports equipment and bicycles available for hire. Some resorts have super indoor pools with exciting features like wave machines, rivers, slides and waterfalls - fun for all ages.

Entrance to the pool complex is included in the cost of the villa rental, but other sports and health facilities must be paid for as taken. Spa areas are open to over 14s only, but family sessions are arranged several times a week so younger children and their parents can enjoy using the saunas and steam rooms together.

A multitude of child-orientated activities keeps all ages happy and safely occupied, leaving parents free to relax. Resorts offer a good range of body and beauty treatments as well as hairdressing services, seven days a week which can be booked in advance.

Accommodation is in self-catering modern villas, fully equipped down to the last teaspoon. Shops within resorts (supermarkets, newsagents, confectionary, sports shops, etc) open early and close late, so shopping for food and other supplies is easy and convenient.

Although resorts are sited in beautiful rural areas with local attractions, many visitors never venture off the site during their entire stay, preferring instead to explore the resort's acres of landscaped grounds, nature trails and paths - on foot, horseback or bicycle.

The health resort is a popular option for parents wanting to combine health facilities and treatments with an enjoyable self-catering family holiday.

PRICE CATEGORIES

The price category letter refers to the lowest price charged per person for accommodation on a nightly basis.

In hotels offering special breaks this is usually the cost per person sharing a double room on a half board basis, ie bed/breakfast and either lunch or dinner.

Where the letter is followed by ✻ the price includes full board and the cost of one or more treatments.

Prices were correct when this book went to press, but all details relating to treatments, facilities and prices should be checked before booking.

Unless otherwise stated, prices include VAT and service charge.

A	£100+
B	£75 - £100
C	£50 - £75
D	£35 - £50
E	£35 or less

SYMBOL KEY

32	Number of bedrooms (number shown in box)
☆	Price includes at least one daily treatment
	Aromatherapy / massage
	Heat treatments
	Beauty treatments
	Hairdressing
	Slimming treatments
	Alternative health treatments
	Medical screening facilities
	No alcohol
	No smoking in public rooms
	Stress management
	Nutritional counselling
	À la carte menus
	Swimming pool
	Open fires in winter
	Outdoor sports facilities
	Gymnasium
	Golf available on site
£	Credit cards accepted

ENGLAND
southern

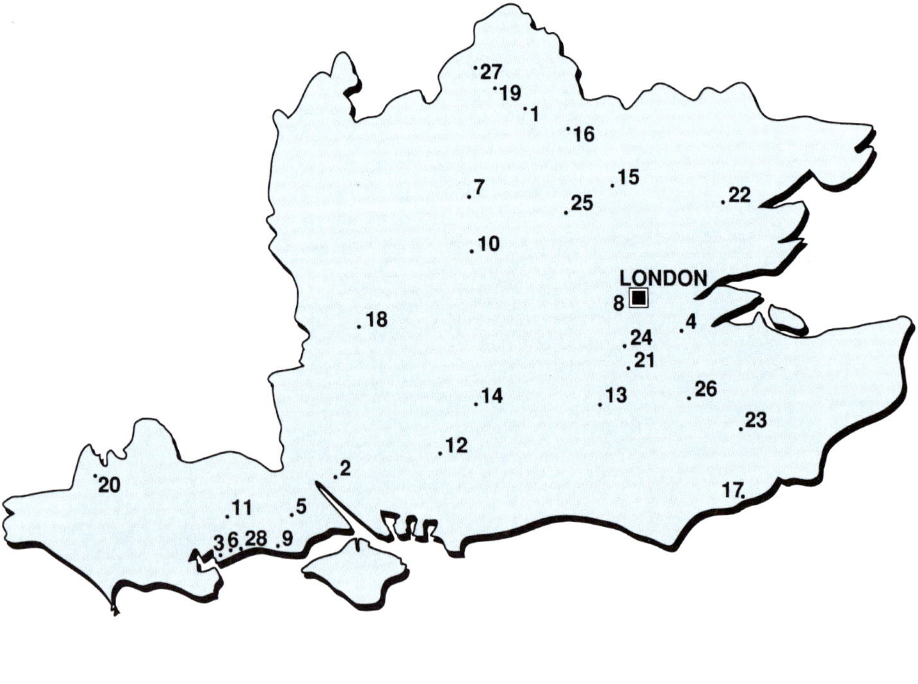

ESTABLISHMENTS IN SOUTHERN ENGLAND

Map ref.		Page no.
1	Beadlow Manor Hotel & Health Farm	18
2	Botley Park Hotel & Country Club	21
3	Bournemouth Centre	23
4	Brandshatch Place	25
5	Careys Manor	27
6	Carlton Hotel	30
7	Champneys	32
8	Champneys London	35
9	Chewton Glen	37
10	Cliveden	40
11	Dormy Hotel	43
12	Forest Mere	45
13	Gatwick Europa	48
14	Grayshott Hall	51
15	Hanbury Manor	54
16	Henlow Grange	57
17	High Glade Natural Spa	60
18	Inglewood Health Hydro	62
19	Malletts Hotel & Health Farm	65
20	Middle Piccadilly	67
21	Nutfield Priory	69
22	Pontlands Park	71
23	Sawyers	73
24	Selsdon Park Hotel	75
25	Sopwell House	77
26	Spa Hotel Tunbridge Wells	80
27	Tyringham	82
28	Verde	85

ENGLAND southern

BEADLOW MANOR
BEDFORDSHIRE

Beadlow Manor Health Farm
Beadlow   Nr Shefford   Bedfordshire   SG17 5PH
ⓒ 0525 60800   (Fx) 0525 61345

30

Price category B✶

Beadlow Manor is situated in rural Bedfordshire overlooking meadows and woodlands and adjoining 300 acres of championship golf courses. Guest facilities are incorporated in three main buildings on the site - the comfortable residential hotel, the country club and health farm, and the distinctive Tapestry restaurant and lounge.
  The Fitz Health and Beauty Club is housed in a purpose designed building, and has a magnificent, large Polaris gym with an extensive array of sophisticated apparatus. No swimming pool at present but there are steam baths, separate saunas, spa bath and jacuzzi, and on the first floor a dance studio, solaria, hairdressing salon, beauty and treatment rooms. A registered osteopath is available for consultation.

The comfortable bedrooms all have en suite bathroom and shower, television, radio, telephone, trouser press and welcome tray.

Breakfast and light meals are served in the Manor, and more formal dining in traditional style from the à la carte and table d'hôte menus in the Tapestry Restaurant.

Beadlow Manor is essentially a golfing oasis - with a new 25 station driving range and two championship 18-hole golf courses. Golf weekends are available and cost £163 per person.

Treatments

The Fitz Health and Beauty Club offers an extensive range of the latest body and beauty treatments and hairdressing, plus nutritional counselling, osteopathic consultations and therapy.

Body treatments:

G5 massage £7 each session, 3 for £19.50 or 6 for £36; Swedish body massage £8, with infra red £10.50; aromatherapy and reflexology £23.50; aromatherapy massage alone £18; body exfoliation £8.50; Cathiodermie bust treatment £16.50; waxing from £3.25.

Beauty treatments:

A full range of René Guinot Cathiodermie treatments are offered, facials from £19.50, eye and neck Cathiodermie £15 each or £26 combined; other facials from £9.50; make-up lesson £8.50; eyebrow and eyelash tint £7; electrolysis from £5 per 1/4 hour; manicure £7.50; pedicure £10.50.

Beadlow Manor specialises in the much acclaimed Ionithermie slimming and facial treatment which uses faradic and galvanic currents and clay in its somewhat messy but effective application. A single session costs £30 or 5 for £120.

Tariff

Special Fitz health weekend breaks include a generous number of treatments and further optional ones can be booked.

The tariff includes accommodation and dinner on Friday and Saturday evenings, two full English breakfasts, sauna, spa bath, steam, gym, snack lunch on Saturday, facial, G5, manicure, Swedish body massage, sunbed and traditional Sunday lunch prior to departure.

The price is £163 per person and is based on two people sharing a twin or double room.

Non-residential days are also available:

The *Health and Leisure Day* costs £60 and includes sauna, steam room, spa bath, sunbed and coffee, massage and pedicure. After lunch, manicure, facial, make-up, use of gym facilities, blow dry or shampoo and set.

The *Day of Beauty* costs £33 and includes sauna, steam room, spa bath and coffee, massage, lunch, sunbed, facial and tea and free use of gym facilities.

Travel Directions
Take M1 motorway and exit at junction 12 or 13 and follow directions to A507 towards Shefford.

Nearest railway station Flitwick approximately 3 miles.

ENGLAND southern

**BOTLEY PARK
HAMPSHIRE**

Botley Park Hotel and Country Club
Winchester Road Botley Hampshire SO3 2UA
☎ 0489 780888   (Fx) 0489 789242

|100|

Price category C   A Rank Character Hotel

This attractive and impressive new development nestles in the rolling Hampshire countryside just a few miles from Southampton. Set in landscaped parklands which include a challenging 18-hole golf course, Botley Park offers weekend and leisure breaks with full use of the extensive health and sporting facilities.

Among amenities at the Country Club of this fine new hotel are a beautiful pool complex with large heated indoor pool and adjoining spa pool, sauna, steam room, and solaria.

Beauty treatment rooms and a hairdressing salon offer a range of body, face and hair treatments.

Sports facilities are excellent with an 18-hole golf course, fully equipped gym, exercise/aerobics suite, two squash courts, snooker room, three tennis courts, petanque terrain, croquet and a putting green.

All bedrooms have modern private bathrooms, television, telephone, hair drier, tea/coffee making facilities and mini-bar (chargeable).

The Winchester Restaurant serves a good choice of table d'hôte and à la carte dishes until 10.00pm. Special diets can usually be catered for on request.

Pre-dinner drinks and bar meals can be taken in either the Gallery Bar or the Swing and Divot Bar overlooking the golf course - bar meals are also served.

Saturday night dinner dances are featured throughout the year and are included in the weekend break packages.

Treatments

A full body massage (ladies only) lasts an hour and costs £18; back, neck and shoulder massage £12; facials from £11; eyelash/eyebrow tint £6; acne treatment face or back £17; make-up from £8; manicure £7; pedicure £9; waxing treatments from £4; electrolysis from £5.50.

A *Day of Beauty* incorporating 4 hours of individually chosen treatments costs £72.

The Cutting Garden hairdressing salon has an impressive selection of hair care; shampoo and set £5.75, perming from £21, highlights/lowlights from £17, etc.

Tariff

Two night weekend breaks at Botley Park cost £113 per person and include accommodation, full English breakfast, table d'hôte dinner, Saturday dinner dance and full use of Country Club amenities.

Travel Directions

From M27 exit at junction 7 and follow signs to Botley for 2 miles, then take B3354 (signposted Fair Oak from the centre of Botley) for 2 miles.

Nearest railway station Southampton approximately 5 miles

ENGLAND southern

**BOURNEMOUTH CENTRE
DORSET**

Bournemouth Centre of Complementary Medicine
26 Sea Road Boscombe Bournemouth Dorset BH5 1DF
☏ 0202 396354   (Fx) 0202 303143

Price category D✵

The Bournemouth Centre of Complementary Medicine is a residential clinic specialising in a wide range of alternative treatments. It is situated on the road to the sea in Boscombe, one of Bournemouth's pleasant suburbs, minutes from the seafront, pier and shopping centre.

Personally supervised and managed by Dr Milo Siewert and his wife Sheila, the Centre provides a caring environment for visitors in need of health restoration, as well as those needing a rest in peaceful surroundings.

All guests have an initial consultation on arrival. Treatments aim to achieve a balance of mind, emotions and bodily functions by boosting the body's natural healing force and restoring vitality and well-being.

Facilities at the Centre include sauna, whirlpool, steam bath, pine, moor and salt baths, massage and solarium.

Menus are totally vegetarian, planned to suit individual needs and use only the best organic produce. Guests can take breakfast in their rooms if they wish.

Single or twin-bedded rooms do not have en suite facilities, but there are five bathrooms and plenty of extra toilets and showers throughout the Centre.

Treatments

Health treatments:

Courses for arthritic patients and cancer counselling are two of several interesting options available at the Bournemouth Centre. Dr Siewert, a medical doctor and osteopath, administers the Kelley Programme, a personalised nutritional programme of metabolic ecology for cancer and degenerative diseases.

As the emphasis is strictly on health and use of alternative medical therapies (guests are referred to as patients), all residents are required to complete an admission form with details of their medical history, so relevant treatments and therapies can be planned.

More than ten practitioners are available to give treatments in various therapies including acupuncture £20; allergy testing £20; colonic irrigation £20; homoeopathy £20; polarity £20; reflexology £7.50.

Chiropractic, cranial osteopathy, dietary therapy, meditation, nutritional counselling, iridology and psychotherapy can be arranged on request.

Body and beauty treatments:

Guests wanting a relaxing time and some pampering can take advantage of the Beauty Room - treatments include Slendertone £5; G5 massage £4.50 per 15 minute session or 5 for £20; aromatherapy facial £10; aromatherapy body massage £18; manicure £4.50; pedicure £6; waxing from £3.50; eyelash tinting £3.50.

Tariff

The daily tariff of £35 to £45 includes massage, exercise and relaxation, talks, sauna, steam and jacuzzi and is inclusive of meals and accommodation. There is a free weekly yoga session.

The weekly rate is £185 per person in a shared double room or £225 per week in a single room.

When residence is longer than three weeks, Saturdays are free of charge.

Travel Directions

From Bournemouth take A35 Christchurch road to Boscombe. Nearest railway station Bournemouth Central 3 miles.

**ENGLAND
southern**

BRANDSHATCH PLACE
KENT

Brandshatch Place
Fawkham   Kent   DA3 8NQ
☎ 0474 872239   Fx 0474 879652

Price category C   A Hidden Hotel

A mellow Georgian building, Brandshatch Place is situated at the end of a long tree-lined avenue amid twelve acres of gardens and woodlands. Such a peaceful setting in the heart of rural Kent makes it an ideal choice for a short relaxing break. The hotel offers elegant surroundings, comfortable en suite bedrooms and friendly service with excellent food and wine.

Visitors have use of Fredericks, the modern leisure club in the grounds adjacent to the hotel. Sports facilities include three squash courts, badminton court, well equipped fitness room with latest hydraulic single station equipment, rowers, cycles and joggers, two full size snooker tables, table tennis, and all weather tennis court with coaching available.

The poolside amenities are equally impressive with a heated swimming pool and separate children's play pool, steam room, sauna, spa pool and two solaria with en suite showers.

Entrance to the pool and gym is free, and only a nominal charge made for use of the other sports and health facilities.

A wide range of fitness and aerobic classes are held throughout the week, full details from the leisure club reception or on the notice board. Personal fitness assessments can be arranged on request and individual exercise programmes worked out.

All comfortable rooms at Brandshatch Place are fully en suite with delightful furnishings and decoration.

Treatments
Body treatments:

A therapy clinic provides a varied range of health, body and beauty treatments, including a 'health farm' half day.

This costs £40 and comprises one heat treatment (sauna, steam bath or spa), 1/2 hour massage, facial and manicure.

Other optional treatments include aromatherapy £20 per hour which may include reflexology; shiatsu therapy and acupressure with essential oils £10; massage including neuromuscular techniques to benefit muscles and nerve pathways £18 per hour or £9 per 1/2 hour - with infra red therapy lamp or audio sonic £5 extra; waxing from £4.

Beauty treatments:

Beauty therapists offer a range of natural skincare facials including Triactive Aroma facial 4 hours £19 - designed for ageing skin and those with premature wrinkles; super lifting facial 1 hour £17; Seborreor facial for problem/teenage skin £17; manicure £6; pedicure £7 or £9.50 with foot and lower leg massage and enamel; eyelash and eyebrow treatments from 4.50; skin care and make-up lesson £15.

Tariff
Special weekend breaks are available from £230 for two people for two nights or £150 for one person staying two nights and are inclusive of overnight accommodation, table d'hôte dinner, English or continental breakfast, newspaper and membership of leisure club during visit.

Regular tariff from £75 single - £90 double (room only).

Continental breakfast £5, English breakfast £7.75, dinner from £17.50.

Travel Directions
From M25 exit at junction 3 (junction 1 of M20), then A25 south to West Kingsdown and Fawkham Green. Hotel is 1/2 mile from village of Fawkham.

Nearest railway station Longfield 2 miles.

CAREYS MANOR
HAMPSHIRE

ENGLAND southern

Careys Manor Hotel
Brockenhurst   Hampshire   SO42 7RH
☏ 0590 23551   (Fx) 0590 22799

| 80 |

Price category C

This lovely, ivy-clad manor is situated in the New Forest, amid five acres of sweeping lawns and attractive, mature trees.

Careys Manor prides itself on giving guests a personal welcome, combining delicious food and comfortable accommodation with some of the most professional and comprehensive facilities available in any hotel leisure complex.

All bedrooms are furnished to a high standard with en suite bathroom, satellite television, telephone, tea/coffee making facilities, bathrobe, hair drier, and trouser press. Most rooms are in the Garden Wing with either a terrace or balcony overlooking the gardens.

This is a popular hotel for honeymoon stopovers, and romantics can request one of the delightful four poster rooms.

Children sharing their parents' room in July and August are accommodated free, at other times a charge of £10 per night is made. A high tea children's menu is available in the restaurant between 6.00pm and 7.00pm

A extensive range of table d'hôte and à la carte menus are served in the pleasant dining room overlooking the gardens.

Hotel residents have full use of the Carat Club with a large ozone swimming pool and jetstream, adjacent jacuzzi, sauna, steam room, impulse shower, solarium and rest area. Aquarobic sessions are held on a regular basis. Children can enjoy the pool and jacuzzi at certain specified times if accompanied by their parents.

Before using the apparatus in the gym, everyone gets a complete heart and lung check-up from head coach Tony Kaspers. The best length and type of exercise is then recommended individually.

Treatments

Body treatments:

Aromatherapy £18 (plus initial consultation £7); full body massage £15; G5 massage £9 or 6 for £45; trimtone toning £9 or 6 for £45.

Beauty treatments:

The Carat Club's beauty department specialises in Cathiodermie, the unique and effective facial treatment created by René Guinot, excellent for problem or wrinkle-prone skin with its unique cleansing action. A Cathiodermie facial costs £17, eye treatment £12, neck £10, back £12 and bust £13. Other beauty treatments include manicure £6; pedicure £8; waxing from £3.50; electrolysis from £3.50.

A new fashion range of make-up by Mary Cohr has recently been introduced, and make-up lessons and demonstrations are held at regular intervals.

A Carat Club's *Top to Toe Beauty* half day includes a selection of treatments and costs £37.

Special treatments:

Unique to Careys Manor is a sports injuries clinic, managed and run by qualified physiotherapists in a fully equipped treatment room with thorough clinical assessment. The clinic is fully approved by private medical health care schemes. Treatments include interferential, ultrasound, transcutaneous nerve stimulation, infra red heat and ice machine.

Individual progressive exercise therapy programmes can be devised.

Tariff
Two night bargain breaks are available throughout the year and include dinner, bed and breakfast. Lunch may be taken instead of dinner.

Rates per person are from £99.70 to £119.70. Bed and breakfast tariff per room (two persons) from £89.90 to £109.90.

Travel Directions
From London take M3 and follow signs to Bournemouth, joining M27 westbound. Exit at junction 1 signposted New Forest. Follow signs to Lyndhurst and Lymington (A337). Enter Brockenhurst and Careys Manor is on the left.

Nearest railway station Brockenhurst less than 1/2 mile.

ENGLAND southern

CARLTON HOTEL
DORSET

The Carlton Hotel
East Overcliff   Bournemouth   Dorset   BH1 3DN
ⓒ 0202 552011   (Fx)   0202 299573

| 65 | ☆ | 🔍 | ≋ | ◉ | ✂ | kg | 📖 | ≋ | ✕ | £ |

Price category B

Located in a prime position on Bournemouth's East Cliff, this independent and luxurious Edwardian hotel offers enjoyable short breaks using the facilities of its health club. These include steam cabinets, sauna, whirlpool spa, solaria and a well equipped gym. Low impact aerobics and yoga classes are available on certain dates.

Healthy low fat/low calorie refreshments are served throughout the day.

The club has its own shop stocked with health and beauty products as well as the latest fashions in fitness clothing.

Unfortunately there is no indoor pool as yet, but the attractive outdoor heated pool is open from April to October, and has a popular sunbathing area with parasols and loungers conveniently accessible from the health club.

All en suite rooms at the Carlton are spacious and luxurious with co-ordinated furnishings and bathroom accessories. Many have spectacular sea views towards the Isle of Wight or Studland Point.

In the evenings a resident pianist plays in the bar where an aperitif can be sipped before trying the varied dishes of the table d'hôte or à la carte menus in the elegant dining room.

Treatments

Body treatments:

Aromatherapy massage £20; G5 massage £14; vacuum suction £10; paraffin body waxing £20; Slendertone £8 per session or £60 for 10; bust improvement treatments from £50.

Beauty treatments:

An extensive number of facial treatments using Decleor and René Guinot products is available and includes Decleor 5-Vitamin facials from £21.50 each; Triactive Aroma (Hollywood facial) £38.50; Superfirming facial £22.50; Seborreor facial £22.95; Cathiodermie £19; Bio-Peel £14; Geloide Prescription facial using jellied flora and herbs £17.

Tariff

Two nights' accommodation, early morning tea and newspaper, full English breakfast, four-course table d'hôte dinner is £158 per double room per night. A full day's health and beauty treatments in the Health Suite costs an additional £65 per person and requires booking at the same time as the accommodation.

Travel Directions

From central Bournemouth follow signs to East Cliff. East Overcliff Drive is on the sea front, east of the pier.

Nearest railway station Bournemouth Central less than a mile.

ENGLAND southern

CHAMPNEYS
HERTFORDSHIRE

Champneys
New Court   Wiggington   Tring   Hertfordshire   HP23 6HY
℡ 0442 863351 & 873153 (reservations)   (Fx) 0442 872342

Price category A✲

Champneys, one of Britain's leading health resorts, is situated in the Chiltern Hills amid 170 acres of attractive parkland, close to the tiny village of Tring in Hertfordshire.

The creeper covered red-brick mansion, once a home of the wealthy Rothschild family, now houses the elegant reception rooms and many of the luxurious bedrooms and suites.

When it opened in 1925, Champneys was the UK's first health resort to operate under full medical supervision. Now owned by Guinness plc, its reputation attracts wealthy visitors from all over the world.

The outstanding facilities - heated indoor swimming pool, whirlpool bath, steam, sauna and outdoor jacuzzi - have recently been extended with a dance studio, squash courts, fully equipped gym, men's spa and new bedrooms.

Outdoor activities include tennis, badminton, croquet, putting, giant chess, golf driving range, as well as bicycling, nature walks and jogging trails.

On arrival everyone has a consultation with a medical adviser and individually designed programmes and diets are arranged. There are programmes to help with particular medical problems such as back pain or cardiovascular disorders, with qualified physiotherapists, dieticians and lifestyle consultants on hand to give advice and treatments.

Medical screening, a stop smoking programme, back care course and stress management can be arranged. With almost 240 staff looking after an average 100 residents, most guests' needs can be covered.

Alternative health treatments are carried out in the Japanese aromatherapy suite, housed in a new complex complete with an interior waterfall. Options available include acupuncture and osteopathy.

Improving individual levels of fitness is an important part of the Champneys' programme via personal assessments with high tech equipment and modern exercise machines in the gym. The latest innovation is a Skier's Edge machine, to help improve fitness prior to a skiing holiday.

The dance studio has a plethora of different types of classes suitable for all levels of fitness, and the beautiful indoor pool provides further opportunities for exercise with swimming lessons and aquarobics classes.

Champneys offers a full activity programme from 8.00am to 10.00pm each day, so there is always something to do or learn about. However guests can relax and do nothing at all, if that is their preference. The myriad of options includes self-hypnosis training, cookery demonstrations, flower arranging, painting, back-care classes, organised walks, lectures or browsing in the well-stocked boutique.

Eating - even dieting - is one of the pleasures of a stay here with a choice of two dining rooms - the Sundial for those fasting or seeking low calorie food, and the adjoining Trellis Room, serving larger portions of exquisitely prepared food of high standard. Dieters can follow a 1,000 calorie a day diet, and non-dieters, vegetarians and those on special medical diets can all be catered for. Unless contra-indicated, one half bottle of wine per day is allowed with lunch or dinner, or shared between the two meals.

Most accommodation is on a par with the best offered in de luxe hotels, but surprisingly there are still some single rooms lacking en suite facilities. Rooms are individually designed with co-ordinating furniture, prints, furnishings, even door and window fittings. Bathrooms are luxurious and some suites have individual jacuzzis.

Treatments

Amenities and treatments included in daily tariff:

Consultations with the Duty Sisters and Dietician, exercise and relaxation classes, lectures, use of the Leisure Craft Centre, sports and recreational facilities, social activities and the following treatments:

1 heat treatment (sauna/plunge, steam or seaweed/pine bath)

Full body massage daily except on day of arrival and Sunday.

Optional body and beauty treatments:

Aromatherapy £43.85; Cathiodermie £32.20; Geloide Prescription facial £22.50; Collagen facial £32.70; Clarins fresh cells rejuvenating course of 5 treatments £128.75; reflexology 19.65; underwater massage £18.35; G5 massage £18.35; Slendertone £12.20; waxing from £5.60; standard manicure £11.75; standard pedicure £12.75; eyebrow and eyelash tint £13.50; low intensity sunbed £8.40; high intensity sunbed £18.35, etc.

An explanatory video is shown from time to time, explaining the facilities and free consultations can be arranged with therapists to create individual programmes.

Tariff

There are eight types of accommodation - all expensive - ranging from a daily tariff of £148 for a basic single room without bathroom to £710 for a premier suite. The lowest daily rate for a single room with en suite bathroom is £215 and for a double £275.

Three day special interest programmes focusing on personal well-being have recently been introduced at Champneys:

Fitness £530 to £542 single - £793 to £838 double;
Beauty £489 to £500 single - £700 to £757 double;
Eating for Health £512 to £525 single - £748 to £803 double;
Lifestyle £537 to £550 single - £799 to £855 double.

Day programmes are also offered at Champneys - *Health and Beauty Day* including seven treatments, lunch or dinner £110; *Health and Fitness Day* including four treatments, lunch or dinner £75 or £105 with fitness assessment.

Travel Directions

Leave M1 at junction 8 and take A41 signposted Hemel Hempstead and Tring for approx 12 miles. At Tring look out for sign to Wiggington and Champneys, approx 2 miles.

Nearest railway stations Tring 5 miles, Berkhamsted 12 miles.

CHAMPNEYS
LONDON

ENGLAND southern

Champneys   The London Club
The Meridien Hotel   Piccadilly   London   W1V 0BH
℡ 071-734 8000 (Hotel)   071-437 8114 (Club)   (Fx) 071-437-3574

Price category A

The Meridien is one of London's leading hotels and is situated in the heart of the West End. Edwardian splendour fused with a sprinkling of French glamour and style give this luxury hotel an unmistakable character and charm.

There are sumptuous lounges, fine restaurants and luxurious rooms with en suite bathroom, television, telephone and trouser press.

All hotel residents have the use of Champneys' exclusive health club which is on site, and includes a stunning swimming pool, Turkish bath, jacuzzi, fully supervised Nautilus gym and indoor golf.

Daily exercise classes are arranged to suit personalised fitness programmes, and there are snooker/billiard tables and two glass backed squash courts. The Club has an Edwardian drawing room for quiet relaxation and a library with daily newspapers and notepaper.

A charming restaurant overlooks the pool and serves breakfast, lunch and dinner seven days a week. The Club is open 18 hours each day throughout the year.

Treatments

A wide range of body and beauty treatments are carried out by experienced staff and these include:

Body massage £30; aromatherapy massage £39; Cathiodermie facial £30; reflexology £25; cleanse/tone/make-up £18; deep cleansing facial £26; manicure £19; pedicure £21.

Slimming treatments are also available and include G5 massage 1/2 hour £15; Slendertone 3/4 hour £15; Dead Sea mud wrap £50; 1/2 hour sunbed treatment £15.

Tariff

Rooms at the Meridien start at £205.65 per night single, £229.15 double, suites from £346.65 to £646.75 per night.

Travel Directions

The Meridien is situated on Piccadilly in central London.
All London mainline railway termini are within short distance.

CHEWTON GLEN
HAMPSHIRE

ENGLAND southern

Chewton Glen
New Milton   Hampshire   BH25 6QS
© 0425 275341(hotel) 0425 277674(health club) (Fx) 0425 272310

Price category B/A

Chewton Glen - privately owned and one of England's leading country house hotels is set in 70 acres of gardens, parklands and woodlands, a ten minute walk from the sea. A superb new Health Club opened in December 1990, further enhancing its enormous appeal.

Martin and Brigitte Skan's exquisite hotel has won many awards and accolades over the years since its purchase in 1966, a Victorian house with eight bedrooms and two bathrooms. Today, Chewton Glen is a renowned hotel with 62 bedrooms and suites all with luxury bathrooms. Any visit here however brief is an unforgettable experience - welcoming and attentive staff, delightful lounges with crackling log fires, welcoming sherry and biscuits in the luxurious bedrooms, high class complimentary toiletries and thick towelling robes in the bathrooms.

Gourmets from all over the world have praised the food served in the Marryat Restaurant, where dinner à la carte costs over £100 for two. Table d'hôte lunch is £22.50 - dinner £39 - both offer an excellent choice of wonderfully cooked and presented food. For guests on a diet, chef Pierre Chevillard can prepare special low calorie menus based on high quality fresh local produce.

Hotel residents have use of the superb new Health Club facilities which include separate saunas, steam room, large spa pool, sunbed, treatment rooms and a fully computerised gym. Individual fitness assessments can be carried out and personally designed programmes devised for use on the latest American gym apparatus.

The magnificent ozone treated swimming pool is a safe 4'6" depth throughout, so can be enjoyed by swimmers and non-swimmers alike. Overlooking the pool is the club's lounge balcony where refreshing juices, tea, coffee and healthy snacks are available on a help yourself basis.

Other amenities include billiard room, outdoor jogging track, 9-hole golf course, outdoor pool and tennis court - two brand new indoor tennis courts for all year round play have recently been constructed, using a continental Marka grain surface, said to lessen fatigue and wear on joints. The indoor courts are housed in a separate complex which is the last word in luxury, with its own changing and shower facilities and car park. Tennis coaching can be arranged and costs £25 per hour.

Treatments

Experienced staff offer a range of therapies and treatments on a par with leading health farms and continental spas, and can advise on individual treatments which are carried out in specially appointed rooms. Following treatments, guests are encouraged to relax for a short period on comfortable recliner chairs in the quietly restful recovery room.

Body treatments:

Full body massage £30; G5 massage £15; French hydrotherapy massage £30; reflexology £30; aromatherapy £40 first visit and consultation, £35 subsequent consultations; Thalgo body and leg wrap using micronised marine algae with selected plant and protein extracts £30; Clarins Paris Method massage treatment for body and bust £40; sunbed treatments from £10; fitness assessment £25; one-to-one personal training £30.

Beauty treatments:

Facials - for men and women from £30; manicure and pedicure £15 each; make-up day/evening £15; eyelash tint £7; waxing from £5.

There is also hairdressing for men and women, with a full range of hair treatments at various prices from £10 for a shampoo/set or a wash/blow dry.

Alternative treatments:

Treatments available by special appointment include full chiropody, osteopathy, homoeopathy, stress management, psychotherapy, naturopathy, shiatsu, nutrition, acupuncture, physiotherapy, Feledenkrais Method and Alexander Technique.

Tariff

Accommodation rates are from £178 per room per night (single or double occupancy), or £243 per room (single or double occupancy) for half board tariff (room, continental breakfast and table d'hôte dinner).

A reduced half board tariff of £215 per room per night applies to stays of five nights or more.

Travel Directions

Take M3 and A33, turning before Southampton onto M27 signposted to Bournemouth. Take A337 to Lyndhurst and follow one-way system onto A35 for Bournemouth. Drive for 10 miles ignoring signs to New Milton, turning left for Walkford and Highcliffe (opposite Cat & Fiddler pub). Continue through Walkford and up Chewton Farm Road.

Nearest railway station New Milton 5 miles.

ENGLAND southern

CLIVEDEN
BUCKINGHAMSHIRE

Cliveden
Taplow   Buckinghamshire   SL6 OJF
☏ 0628 668561   (Fx) 0628 661837

Price category B/A

Famous Cliveden, former home of royalty and the Astor family is the only Grade I listed stately home in Britain offering a full range of health, leisure and sporting activities.

Situated on the banks of the Thames in 376 acres of gardens and parklands, Cliveden was built in 1666 for the 2nd Duke of Buckingham by William Winde - his original terrace still remains on the south facade. The house was bequeathed to the National Trust by the Astor Family, and in 1984 was skilfully transformed into a sumptuous and palatial hotel with splendid public rooms furnished with tapestries, antiques and fine works of art.

All the spacious and luxurious rooms are for double occupancy but can be let as single rooms when required. Several palatial suites are also available.

Guests have a choice of dining rooms - the Terrace Dining Room open daily for lunch and dinner, Waldo's - open Tuesday to Saturday for dinner and the French Dining Room for breakfast and private lunch and dinner parties.

Light lunches and salads are also served in the Pavilion, Cliveden's newly completed spa and country club.

The many sporting facilities available include indoor and outdoor heated swimming pools, squash court, one indoor and two all-weather tennis courts, croquet, boating, horse riding and golf practise holes.

Walking is another activity at Cliveden, with a series of walks laid out through the estate. To maximise the enjoyment of the walks through the spectacular gardens, a special audio tape and Walkman is available for hire.

The Pavilion is situated within a walled garden adjacent to the Mansion and features a 60' indoor pool, large steam room, separate saunas, plunge pool, Canadian hot tub, spa bath with underwater massage, swim jet trainer, solarium, air conditioned gym and four treatment rooms for health, body and beauty treatments.

Treatments

A wide range of body, beauty and alternative health treatments are available.

Body treatments:

Aromatherapy £32; Swedish massage £25; body exfoliation £15; percussion massage £15 per 30 mins; cellulite treatment using Aromazone machine £10 per session; back, neck and shoulder massage £15 per 30 mins.

Beauty treatments:

Cliveden facial for men £30; Cathiodermie £32; Geloide Prescription facial £25; deep skin cleanse £20; cleanse and make-up £20; electrolysis and electrotherapy (to remove skin tags and broken capillaries) from £15.

Other treatments:

Alternative therapies available by special appointment include reflexology, shiatsu, osteopathy, colour therapy, etc.

Fitness assessments, personalised training programmes and instruction on correct use of the modern equipment are offered in the self-contained gym, with its own changing rooms and showers.

Tariff

A fee of £3.80 is levelled on all rooms by The National Trust.

Cliveden's nightly tariff is £208 per double room and includes breakfast and use of most leisure facilities (treatments extra).

Several short break packages are offered:

Relaxation, Fitness and Fun - a three day programme of light exercise and treatments with two nights' accommodation, breakfast, lunch, choice of 3 treatments and 4 light gym sessions. This break is offered for a minimum of two nights, any night except Saturday and costs £105 per guest per night.

Weekend Relaxation, Fitness and Fun from £155 per guest, per night.

The Clivedon Weekend - two nights' accommodation, breakfast, lunch, dinner and choice of treatments from £650 per couple.

Travel Directions

Only 25 miles from London, and easily reached from M4, exit at junction 7, or the M40 junction 2. Cliveden is on the B476, 2 miles north of Taplow. The main gates are opposite The Feathers Public House.

Nearest railway stations Taplow 2 miles, Maidenhead 4 miles.

DORMY HOTEL
DORSET

ENGLAND southern

The Dormy Hotel
New Road Ferndown Dorset BH22 6ES
📞 0202 872121   (Fx) 0202 895388

Price category C   A De Vere Luxury Hotel

This friendly hotel is set in 12 acres of landscaped gardens on the edge of the New Forest adjoining the Ferndown Championship Golf Course. Log fires, oak panelled lounges and bars create a warm and relaxed atmosphere.

Guests have a choice of traditional style rooms and suites (four posters available) or modern style rooms, some adjoining for family use. All bedrooms have en suite bathroom, satellite television, telephone, tea/coffee making facilities, trouser press and hair drier.

Leisure facilities at the Dormy Hotel are excellent - large heated indoor pool, spa bath, saunas, solaria, steam room, computerised gym with instruction, dance studio, two squash courts, all weather tennis court, putting green, golf driving net and snooker - all free to hotel residents.

Gym induction courses are available to those using the high tech equipment for the first time, and individual fitness programmes can be arranged.

The dance studio has an exciting programme of classes and activities throughout the week, including gentle keep fit, aerobics - beginners and advanced, yoga, self defence, martial arts and circuit training.

Aquarobic classes and held in the swimming pool.

Guests are encouraged to join in the classes, there's even a timetable in all rooms - book in advance to secure a place.

Treatments

In a new health and beauty department, experienced therapists use an extensive range of products and treatments. The choice includes:

Aromatherapy - full body and facial £30; G5 massage £6; Slendertone £6 or £50 for 6 sessions; body massage £14; body scrub and oils £7; facials from £7.50; manicure £6.50; pedicure £7.75; waxing/electrolysis from £3.25.

A half day *Touch of Luxury* costs £45 and comprises full body massage, basic facial, manicure, body scrub and oils, make-up and lunch.

Tariff

Special two night or weekend breaks which include free use of the leisure club facilities (treatments extra) are available all year round.

These include accommodation and table d'hôte dinne on the first night, full English breakfast and table d'hôte dinner on the second night and full English breakfast and luncheon the following day.

The cost of the break is £133 per person or £266 per couple.

Travel Directions

Within easy reach of M4 or M3, then take A33 to M27. Exit at junction 1 and continue down A31 to Ferndown, turning left at roundabout after Smugglers Inn.

Nearest railway station Bournemouth 6 miles.

FOREST MERE
HAMPSHIRE

ENGLAND southern

Forest Mere
Liphook   Hampshire   GU30 7JQ
℡ 0428 722051   Fx 0428 723501

Price category C✻   Member of the Savoy Hotels Group

This peacefully situated health farm is located at the end of a long private drive which winds through woodlands and around a picturesque lake.

Although the staff are friendly, the approach to health and stress management is serious - no alcohol is allowed, and guests are encouraged to avoid business and social pressures and limit their driving during the period of their stay. It is essentially a quiet haven for relaxation and unwinding.

An initial consultation discusses medical background and lifestyle, so a beneficial programme of treatments, diet and exercise can be planned.

The tariff includes a daily sauna or steam bath with therapeutic massage and osteopathy if required, as well as use of the sporting amenities and exercise classes.

There is a pleasantly warm (if rather small) indoor swimming pool and a beautifully sheltered outdoor pool surrounded by gardens and sunbathing terraces - heavenly in the heat of the summer.

Classes for most levels of fitness are held in the purpose built exercise studio, alongside the supervised gym. Other activities available include tennis, badminton, boating on the lake, bicycles, snooker, billiards, table tennis and a nature trail with fitness stations.

The daily schedule of treatment times, newspaper and the morning's post are served alongside breakfast in bed each morning. All other meals are served in Forest Mere's two restaurants which produce a delicious selection of fresh and nourishing meals.

In the Light Diet Room freshly made soups, fruit and home-made yoghurt are served for lunch and supper. The main Dining Room has a buffet lunch with a choice of salads, fresh fruit and yoghurt, and more substantial meals in the evening.

No alcohol intake by residents is allowed, on or off the premises. Guests contravening this rule will be asked to leave. This underlines the serious approach to correct diet and self discipline in Forest Mere's aim to help achieve rest, lifestyle improvement and stress control.

There are no signed celebrity pictures smiling down from the walls here, Forest Mere is far too discreet for that sort of publicity. Perhaps that is why it has more than its fair share of well known visitors including royalty every year.

Treatments

Body and beauty treatments:

A long list of optional body and beauty treatments for male and female guests is available and can be booked in advance.

Cathiodermie facial £30.50; back Cathiodermie £38; Bio-Peel £20; Clarins facial £20; Paris Method facial £30; Paris Method body massage £31; seaweed body treatment for women £22; waxing from £4.50; eyelash dye £8.50; eyelash and eyebrow dye £11.

Other treatments:

Forest Mere has a fully equipped physiotherapy department, and can offer interferential therapy, ultrasonics, faradism, wax baths, hydrotherapy and infra red treatments. Guests wishing to take advantage of these treatments should ask their own doctor to write to the physician at Forest Mere.

Physiotherapy charges can be claimed back on some health insurance policies when supported by a doctor's certificate.

Tariff

The choice and price of rooms at Forest Mere is somewhat confusing, with five different categories of bedroom to choose from.

All rooms have wash-basin, television, telephone and electric blanket, and some rooms have wc, shower and bidet.

Arrival and departure are on Sunday and Wednesday only. Visitors are asked to arrive in the afternoon and leave immediately after lunch on day of departure.

Prices start at £210 for a basic room for a 3-day stay; £490 per week; (daily rate £70).

The most expensive rooms cost £480 for a 3-day stay; £1,120 per week; (daily rate £160).

Travel Directions

Forest Mere is 2 miles south west of Liphook on the A3 London - Portsmouth road, 48 miles from London.

Nearest railway stations Liphook 2 miles and Haslemere. 7 miles.

ENGLAND southern

GATWICK EUROPA HOTEL
WEST SUSSEX

Gatwick Europa Hotel
Balcombe Road Maidenbower Nr Crawley West Sussex RH10 4ZR
⊙ 0293 886666   (Fx) 0293 886680

| 211 |

Price category C

This attractive new hotel is designed in hacienda style and set in more than six acres of Sussex countryside with landscaped gardens and mature trees. The whitewashed walls and terracotta roof create a Spanish flavour echoed indoors with a wealth of exotic plants, terrazzo and marble floors and dark mahogany furniture. Because of the unusual low lying design of the building, 75 of the 211 rooms are on the ground floor.

Hotel residents have complimentary use of Studio 4, the hotel's private health and fitness club, which incorporates a comprehensive range of the latest facilities for pleasant relaxation or vigorous exercise.

range of the latest facilities for pleasant relaxation or vigorous exercise.

Amenities include a 12 metre heated indoor pool, sauna, steam room, sunbeds, spa bath, dance studio with full range of classes to suit all levels of fitness.

Studio 4 also has a juice bar, sun lounge with relaxation area, conservatory lounge, a computerised gym, hairdressing and treatment rooms. Treatments are available Tuesday to Saturday.

The modern en suite bedrooms are spacious with furnishings and decoration echoing the Spanish theme. All rooms have television, telephone, mini-fridge, tea/coffee making facilities, trouser press, hair drier and bathroom scales. Non-smoking, disabled and special ladies' rooms (offering complete security and additional amenities such as iron and ironing board) are available on request.

Three restaurants, including the Silk Trader, a stylish Chinese à la carte restaurant, cater for all tastes and appetites. The Mediterranée provides European and exotic North African dishes. Buffet lunches and a good selection of food in the evening is served in the Conservatory.

Car parking is free whilst in residence, and £3 daily thereafter. A courtesy coach service runs to and from Gatwick airport, just six miles away.

Treatments

Body treatments:

Ionithermie slimming treatment £30.00 (course of 5 treatments recommended); back, neck and shoulder massage £10.95; aromatherapy body massage £25.00.

Beauty treatments:

Decleor aromatherapy products are used in a variety of facials including the Vitamin 5 programme suitable for all types of skin. The range consists of Cleoderm, Revitalising, Remodelling, Hydrating and Aromadermy and each facial costs £20.50. The Decleor Seborreor facial for problem skins £20.50 and the Triactive Aroma (Hollywood facial) for mature skins and premature lines £31.50 are also available.

Eyelash tinting £6.95; manicure from £6.95; pedicure £10.95; waxing from £3.50; electrolysis £4.25 for 10 minutes.

Hairdressing is available from £5.75.

A *Top to Toe* half day costs £56 and includes aromatherapy massage, full facial, eyebrow tidy, manicure, pedicure, make-up, wash and

blow dry - a great start or finish to a holiday!
Tariff

A special health package is available costing £166 per person and includes:
Overnight accommodation and breakfast for two nights with full use of Studio 4 Health Club.
Top to Toe beauty treatment (four hours of pampering including aromatherapy massage, full facial, eyebrow tidy, manicure, pedicure, make-up, wash and blow-dry).

The regular tariff is from £100 per room (one or two persons) and does not include breakfast.

Executive rooms cost £120 per night and can accommodate parents and up to two children.

Travel Directions
From M23 motorway exit at junction 10 and turn onto B2036 Balcombe Road. The hotel is 5 minutes from motorway exit and approximately 2 miles from centre of Crawley.

Nearest railway stations Crawley 2 miles, Three Bridges 1 mile.

GRAYSHOTT HALL
SURREY

ENGLAND southern

Grayshott Hall Health and Fitness Resort
Headley Road Grayshott Nr Hindhead Surrey GU26 6JJ
☏ 0428 604331   (Fx) 0428 605463

| 75 |

Price category A✶

This established health farm is situated in some of Surrey's most picturesque National Trust countryside. The well-preserved Victorian house is surrounded by 47 acres of gardens with lakes and immaculately manicured lawns, and is only an hour's drive from London.

Visitors have unlimited use of Grayshott Hall's varied sporting and leisure activities, including 9-hole golf course, outdoor and indoor tennis courts (2 new indoor courts have recently been built), gym, outdoor badminton (summer only), indoor and outdoor swimming pools and jacuzzi.

The daily tariff includes a choice of heat treatment (steam cabinet or sauna) and a daily massage (not Sundays).

Ladies' and men's treatment areas are now comfortably situated within a central atrium, with a new hydrotherapy centre, six additional beauty rooms and a new hairdressing salon.

A new spa area has recently been added and greatly improves the amenities. Hydrotherapy baths and thalassotherapy treatments are now offered, as well as a floatation room. A new steam room has also been opened, which can be enjoyed free of charge.

The daily exercise sessions are open to everyone, and are suitable for all levels of fitness and ability. Classes are held in a pleasant and airy studio and feature yoga, circuit training, stamina development, tummy trimmers, wake up and stretch, rebounders, stretch and relax classes, etc. A class for everyone! Current timetables are on the notice board in the treatment and reception area and in all rooms.

Food is one of the pleasures of a stay at Grayshott Hall with delicious meals made from home-grown fruit, salads and vegetables and prime local produce. Food is attractively presented and plentiful - the piping hot home-made soup is especially good at lunchtime.

Breakfast is served in one's room and other meals are taken in either the Conservatory (calorie controlled diets) or the Dining Room. Lunch is a buffet of calorie counted salads with some hot dishes, and dinner a choice of menus served more formally.

A refreshment bar with free freshly made coffee, tea and other drinks is open at all times.

Evening talks, demonstrations and discussion groups are held regularly, and partners for bridge or tennis can be acquired by advertising on the notice board in the treatments reception lounge.

Daytime dress is informal - tracksuits, trainers and leisure wear - most guests wear ordinary clothes at dinner.

On arrival everyone has an initial personal consultation with a qualified member of staff (usually a nursing sister), who checks blood pressure and gives dietary advice. A suggested programme of treatments and activities is then suggested.

Treatments

Body treatments:
Extensive choice includes aromatherapy £36; reflexology £20; G5 massage £16; oriental body conditioning treatment £55; herbal body wrap £28; Vital Harmony exfoliation £28; floatation £25.

Beauty treatments:
Facials from £23; Cathiodermie from £22; make-up £15; eyelash tint £8; manicure £14; full luxury pedicure £18; waxing from £6; hair and scalp treatments from £12.

Hydrotherapy treatments:
Hydrotherapy bath with underwater massage £35; seaweed wrap £30; blitz jet £20.

The different benefits of the various types of treatments can be explained by staff, making choice easier.

Other amenities:
Special weekends have been organised by Jayne Roberts designed to put stress into prospective. Informal sessions are run by experts in the field of stress management, developing techniques to make significant lifestyle changes. The weekend starts with dinner on Friday, finishing after lunch on Sunday. Special weekend break price of £294 includes accommodation, all meals, massage, two heat treatments, use of all facilities and the stress workshop and notes.

Grayshott Hall is a popular and well organised health farm - it is advisable to book well in advance for both accommodation and extra treatments.

Tariff

Three types of accommodation are available at the following nightly rates:

Main wing basic room (with wash-basin and wc) £121 single or sharing double room £97 per person. Basic room with shower £133 single, or sharing double room £109 per person;
Century wing - superior double rooms with shower £121 per person;
Main house - superior double rooms with bath £109 to £190 per person.

Travel Directions

Take A3 London to Portsmouth road as far as Hindhead. Drive through the village and turn right onto B3002 to village of Grayshott. Grayshott Hall is on the left 1 1/2 miles after the village.

Nearest railway station Haslemere 5 miles.

**ENGLAND
southern**

HANBURY MANOR
HERTFORDSHIRE

Hanbury Manor
Thundridge Nr Ware   Hertfordshire   SG12 OSD
📞 0920 487722   (Fx) 0920 487692

| 98 | ★ | 🏞 | ♨ | ◉ | ✂ | 🇰6 | 📖 | ≋ | 🦆 | 🔍 | ✕ | ⛳ | £ |

Price category A   A Rockresort

Hanbury Manor is a magnificent baronial manor transformed into an exclusive country house hotel with superb health, leisure and beauty facilities, on a par with the best available at any health farm.

The Jacobean style manor was originally built in 1890 for the Hanbury family, and until recently was an exclusive girls' convent and boarding school. Set in 200 acres of Hertfordshire countryside with delightful woodland and meadow walks, there are acres of spectacular gardens to explore with a special walled garden and a 'secret garden'.

Everything about Hanbury Manor is outstanding - luxurious rooms with beautiful bathrooms, toiletries and bathrobes, imaginative food from a choice of three restaurants, sumptuously furnished public rooms with oak panelling and tapestries, enormous log fires, numerous plants and dried flower arrangements and exceptionally friendly staff.

All bedrooms are tastefully furnished and decorated and have luxury bathroom, television, telephone, fridge with mini-bar, hair drier, bathrobes and trouser press. Some rooms have four poster beds.

All this and more - a state of the art Health and Fitness Club housed in a new wing and skilfully designed to complement the Jacobean style architecture. Amenities include a spectacular indoor swimming pool, squash courts, Polaris equipped gym with experienced staff on hand to help and supervise, mirrored aerobics and dance studio with fully sprung floor, sauna and steam rooms, jacuzzi, solarium, games room and comfortable changing and locker facilities with copious supplies of towels.

Outside are three all weather tennis courts, croquet lawns, fitness jogging trail and an 18-hole championship golf course designed by Jack Nicklaus II.

Treatments

Health and beauty treatments are taken in the relaxed surroundings of the Health Club's six treatment rooms with three aromatherapy baths, hand painted ceiling murals and mood music.

Body treatments:

An extensive choice includes: Aroma massage £30; massage £26; G5 massage £18 per 1/2 hour; Vital Harmony exfoliation treatment £30; aroma wrap slimming treatment £30; sunbed £7; aroma bath £6; bust firming treatment £30 or 6 for £160.

Beauty treatments:

Decleor holistic facials £30 each; Aromadermy £35; complete aromatherapy programme £145; Triactive Aroma facial for mature skin £50; waxing from £6; make-up £16; eyelash tinting £9; electrolysis from £9; hairdressing from £7.

Tariff

Two night health and beauty breaks with arrival on any day cost £280 single or £210 per person sharing. This includes accommodation in Executive room for two nights, full English breakfast, table d'hôte dinner in Vardon Grill nightly, one treatment per person daily, fitness evaluations, personal workouts and full use of Health Club facilities.

Non-residential one day health and beauty packages are also offered at Hanbury Manor.

A *Top to Toe Rejuvenation Day* costs £150 and includes massage, body treatment, facial, lunch from Vardon Grill, cut and blow dry, manicure with wax treatment, make-up application or solarium.

A *Complete Health/Beauty/Fitness Day* costs £100 and includes a fitness assessment or lifestyle evaluation, fitness workout, solarium, lunch from Vardon Grill, massage, facial, cut and blow dry.

Travel Directions
From M25 exit at junction 25 and take A10 Cambridge road to Ware. Hanbury Manor is 4 miles north of Ware, 25 miles from London.
Nearest railway station Ware 4 miles.

ENGLAND southern

HENLOW GRANGE
BEDFORDSHIRE

Henlow Grange Health Farm
Henlow   Bedfordshire   SG16 6DP
☎ 0462 811111   Fx 0462 815310

Price category C✻

Henlow Grange is a spacious red brick Georgian manor house set in the countryside 40 miles from London. The grounds include an elegant garden with tennis courts and a winding stream complete with waterfall, but are not large enough for a satisfying walk.

Now owned and managed by the Purdew family, Henlow Grange has been established for 25 years and prides itself on offering a complete fitness and exercise programme for every age, along with an extensive choice of body, slimming, hairdressing and beauty treatments.

All guests have a brief consultation on arrival to work out a personalised fitness programme and choice of treatments. Little or no advice on nutrition is given, but a diet consultation can be arranged as an optional extra for £17.50.

Fitness and sports facilities include indoor heated swimming pool, gym with Nautilus equipment and instruction, exercise bikes and individual trampoline rebounders, exercise studio, tennis (floodlit court), table tennis, badminton, croquet, golf practice net and boats.

The quiet villages in the area are worth exploring by bicycles provided free from reception (mountain bikes can also be hired at extra charge plus deposit of £150!).

All visitors can join in as much as they wish of the exercise and relaxation programmes, which include classes in jazz ballet, aerobics, men's workouts, yoga, relaxation, supervised jogs and walks, gym instruction and body alignment. Talks, demonstrations and make-up classes are frequently held in the evenings.

Breakfast (cereal and fruit) is served in one's room at 7.30am. Lunch is a buffet salad with a hot main course; dinner - a choice of several main dishes, ordered in advance. A glass or two of wine with lunch or dinner is allowed if a strict diet regime is not being followed. Coffee and tea are served throughout the day.

Track suits are usually discarded in favour of smarter clothes at dinner, and there are opportunities to make new friends and share the day's experiences in the coffee bar which stays open until late. Henlow Grange has an easy, relaxed atmosphere, and enjoys promoting its popularity with celebrities from the sporting and show biz world - the walls are covered in signed photos.

Most bedrooms at Henlow Grange have private bathroom, all have colour television and are reasonably well appointed.

Treatments

The range of optional body and beauty treatments is extensive (Henlow Grange has its own training school for beauty therapists) and a new Clarins salon and Manicure/Pedicure room have recently opened.

Body treatments:

Aromatherapy £28.50; faradic toning £10.50; special wax bath £20; Decleor treatments from £23; G5 massage £8; seaweed bath £23; sunbed £5; Swedish body massage £14.50 and many more. Toning tables have recently been installed - sessions last an hour and cost £9.50 each.

Beauty treatments:

Cathiodermie treatments from £23; Clarins Paris Method treatment £28.50; make-up £11.50; hand-waxing £8.50; pedicure £18; wash and blow dry £10.50 (in hairdressing salon) and many more.

Tariff

The nightly tariff per person includes full body massage, facial (or neck/shoulder massage), sauna or Turkish bath as well as full use of all sporting amenities, complete exercise and relaxation programmes, evening demonstrations, lectures, etc.

Economy room without bathroom £79.50 single or £65 per person shared.

Standard room with bath or shower £92.50 single or £75 per person shared.

Premier room £120 single or £89.50 per person shared.

Long weekends are also organised arriving Friday 2.00pm onwards and departing on Sunday around 4.00pm (Rooms must be vacated by 11.00am - however, but changing facilities are made available.)

Weekend includes 1 full body massage, 1 facial (or neck/shoulder massage), 1 G5 massage, full fitness programme and use of all facilities.

Weekend costs from £129.50 - £225.00 per person.

All accommodation includes standard breakfast, buffet luncheon (Sunday lunch is also included) and dinner.

Many other special breaks are offered at Henlow Grange during the year, so telephone for the latest newsletter and details.

Non-residential *Top to Toe* days costing £57.50 are available Monday to Friday - the day includes introductory talk with coffee, sauna and steam, Swedish body massage, dance exercise class, G5 massage, three course lunch, use of swimming pool, gym and sports facilities, pedicure or manicure and facial.

Tea and coffee are served throughout the day.

Travel Directions

Take motorway A1(M) and exit at junction 10, then A507 north to Henlow for 4 miles.

(Ask for detailed directions when booking as brochure map is vague and difficult to follow.) Approach road has cattle grids.

Nearest railway stations Hitchin 1 1/2 miles and Arlesley 1 1/2 miles.

ENGLAND southern

**HIGH GLADE
EAST SUSSEX**

High Glade Natural Health Spa Centre
9 Upper Church Road St Leonards-on-Sea East Sussex TN37 7AT
✆ 0424 753121

Price category C✳

A warm and relaxing welcome awaits all guests at High Glade in this attractive part of East Sussex, with opportunities for invigorating walks along the sea shore or over the South Downs.

High Glade is a serious (but friendly) centre specialising in natural health treatments, and caters for guests seeking relief from stress as well as health improvement generally.

The Centre is privately owned and managed by two resident principals, June Leech and Miriam Eastaugh, both qualified naturopaths/osteopaths and actively involved in the day to day programme of treatments.

Guests are accommodated in High Glade house - a lovely old Victorian residence which has been completely refurbished and is situated in its own grounds with mature trees and lawns.

Bedrooms are attractively furnished in Victorian style and offer spacious mostly en suite accommodation.

Dress is strictly casual and comfortable; track or leisure suits are most convenient, as formal dress is not required at any time. Bring towelling robe, swimwear, bathing cap and soft soled shoes for wearing in the treatment areas.

All guests have an initial consultation with one of the resident practitioners to assess health and individual nutritional needs. Treatments are carried out in the new spa clinic equipped with the most modern facilities available for naturopathic healing.

Where possible, organically grown food is used - all cuisine is vegetarian and carefully prepared.

Treatments

After breakfast (served in bedroom or dining room) visitors walk 50 yards up the drive to the clinic for treatments - steam room or cabinet and sauna; aromatherapy; massage; herbal baths; Scottish douche (alternative hot and cold shower); arm, foot and hip baths. Essences and essential oils can be incorporated into treatments to help many conditions.

Other alternative therapies practised at High Glade include osteopathy, phytotherapy (herbal treatments), reflex zone therapy, yoga and hydrotherapy utilising a full range of therapeutic bath sizes. Beauty therapy, colonic irrigations and vega testing by arrangement.

No treatments are carried out on Sundays.

Tariff

Three weeks' length of stay is the maximum, with one or two week visits recommended - the weekly tariff includes:

2 aromatherapy treatments, 2 osteopathic or massage treatments, 2 sauna or steam baths, 2 herbal baths, 2 Scottish douches.

The weekly rate (Sunday - arrival between 4.00pm and 6.00pm - departure by 11.00am Saturday) is £370 - £460 single; £420 - £440 per person sharing a twin-bedded room; £410 per person sharing a double bedded room.

Two night breaks from £110 - £135 per person; nightly rate £55 - £67.50 per person.

Discounted rates are sometimes offered, so enquire before booking.

Travel Directions

High Glade is in a quiet part of St Leonards-on-Sea, off A21 London road (High Glade is fifth turning on right after DIY store).

Nearest railway station St Leonards (Warrior Square) 1 1/2 miles.

ENGLAND southern

INGLEWOOD HYDRO
BERKSHIRE

Inglewood Health Hydro
Kintbury   Berkshire   RG15 0SL
☏ 0488 682022   (Fx)   0488 682022

| 71 | ☆ | 🖋 | ♨ | ◉ | ✂ | Kg | ◐ | 🍷 | ✗ | ☺ | 🍇 | ≋ | ⚜ | 🔍 | 🚶 | £ |

Price category C✳

Inglewood's history dates back to the days of the 12th century Crusades when it was one of the great houses of the Knights Templar. Today the historic mansion, set in 50 acres of Berkshire countryside, is one of Britain's leading health hydros with a wide range of medical, fitness, beauty and dietary programmes to suit everyone.

  Visitors come to lose weight, gain vitality, or simply to take a break from life's pressures. Post-operative patients and general medical convalescents are welcomed, as are tired mothers of babies and young children. A special arrangement with the famous Norland Nursery just two miles away provides care and a personal nanny for young children of Inglewood's visitors, enabling parents to enjoy a carefree stay.

All visitors have a personal consultation on arrival with friendly and efficient Tini Carson, Matron at Inglewood, who prescribes an individual programme of diet, treatments and exercise. Full clinical investigations can be arranged including cardiac profile assessments, ECG tests, full biochemical and blood analysis, X-ray facilities, physiotherapy and osteopathy.

Weight loss and diet are specialities at Inglewood. Advice from the resident dietician is free, with diets devised to suit personal needs and lifestyles. Guests can opt for a 48 hour lemon and water fast, strict 500 calories a day choices in the light diet room, or calorie counted salads and hot meals in the main dining room. A limited amount of alcohol is served in the main dining room on Friday and Saturday evenings.

Sporting and leisure amenities include croquet, tennis, clock golf, jogging, cycling, jacuzzi, indoor swimming pool, gym and dance studio. Daily classes are held in the exercise studio, gym and indoor pool.

Inglewood's spacious interior is tastefully decorated reflecting the ambience of a stately home with gracious public rooms including a lounge with open fire. The gardens are a delight and well worth exploring, as is the surrounding area with its quaint little villages.

The minimum length of stay is three days. All bedrooms have telephone, radio and television, and most have en suite bath or shower.

There are 71 bedrooms in the main house plus a separate five bedroomed lodge in the grounds.

Treatments

All residential stays include four free treatments daily (none on Sundays, two on midweek arrival and departure days) and chosen from a wide range - further optional treatments can also be taken at the following prices:

Body treatments:

G5 massage £6.65; sauna or steam cabinet £5.85 each; peat bath £5.85; Slendertone £6.65; physiotherapy from £9.40; osteopathy £14.10; massage £15.35; aroma oil bath £5.85. Other options are solarium £4.70 or £23.50 for 6; aromatherapy £32.70 and reflexology £17.35.

Beauty treatments:

Facials from £23 (men's facial £20); eyelash tinting £8; manicure £13.50; pedicure £16.50; waxing from £7.50; electrolysis from £8. A full range of deep penetrating specialist treatments from Decleor are available from £20. Hairdressing starts at £9.50.

The appointments system works well - the spa treatment rooms are around the pool and in the mornings everyone relaxes on poolside loungers awaiting the therapists' call.

Tariff

Nightly accommodation rates start at £62 single *budget* room - £58 per person sharing twin *budget* room with no bathroom (one week bookings only).

Economy single room with shower and wc costs £305 for a three night stay (single rooms only in this category).

Standard room with shower and wc costs £325 single or £268 per person sharing a twin room for a three night stay.

The most expensive accommodation is in the *Inglefield Suite* - this costs £199 per night for single occupancy or £160 per person sharing.

Travel Directions

Kintbury is just off the A4 Hungerford to Newbury road, not far from junction 13 of M4.

Nearest railway station Kintbury 1 mile (free collection) or Newbury 7 miles.

MALLETTS HOTEL
BEDFORDSHIRE

ENGLAND southern

Malletts Hotel and Health Farm
Silsoe Road   Maulden   Bedfordshire   MK45 2AZ
   0525 840400   0525 406459

Price category D

Malletts country house hotel was built in 1815 for the Duke of Bedford, and acquired by present owners Lyn and Ray Mallett in 1984. The Malletts transformed the listed building into a select hotel and health farm which they hope to expand in size in the future.

All the comfortable bedrooms are spacious and individually designed with en suite bathroom, television and telephone.

A comfortable lounge and a cosy bar with open fire are an inducement to relaxation after using the Country Club or for pre-dinner drinks.

The Club's health and fitness facilities are housed in a separate annexe and include an attractive heated indoor swimming pool with therapy jet exerciser, sauna, sunbed and fully equipped and supervised gymnasium.

Sports facilities outdoors include a 6-hole putting green, golf practice nets, and an all weather tennis court.

Malletts has a coffee shop open seven days a week for light meals and an à la carte restaurant for more formal lunches and dinners.

Treatments

A full range of body and beauty treatments and hairdressing is offered in the beauty salon using French GM Collin beauty products.

Body treatments:

Aromatherapy combined with reflexology £28; aromatherapy £24; full body massage £18.50; shoulder and back massage £10; G5 massage £9.50 per session, £50 for course of 6; faradic muscle toning £9.50 per session, £50 for course of 6; body exfoliation and tanning treatment £24.50; sunbed £4; sauna £5; waxing from £4.50; electrolysis from £6.50.

Beauty treatments:

Facials from £13; masque facial with ozone treatment massage £19; seaweed Algomask £24.50; Ultra Derm deep cleansing electronic facial £20; Biologie facial £29.50; eyelash tint £5.50; make-up lesson £19.50; light day make-up £8; manicure £9; pedicure £12.50.

A full range of hairdressing services includes specialised perms and colouring/highlighting treatments.

Tariff

Special leisure breaks are available throughout the year (treatments extra) based on two persons sharing a room:

Dinner, bed and breakfast £50 per person for one night, £95 per person for two nights, £140 per person for three nights and £180 per person for four nights.

Regular room only tariff is from £39 single or £62.50 double (two persons).

Continental breakfast £4.95 - full English breakfast £7.95.

Travel Directions

Take M1 to junction 13 then A507 towards Ampthill and B530 to Maulden.

Nearest railway station Flitwick approximately 1 1/2 miles.

MIDDLE PICCADILLY
DORSET

ENGLAND southern

Middle Piccadilly Natural Healing Centre
Holwell   Sherborne   Dorset   DT9 5LW
☏   0963 23468

Price category D✳

Middle Piccadilly Natural Healing Centre is a 17th century thatched farmhouse set in the pretty Dorset countryside, and offers a uniquely restful break in lovely surroundings.

There is a sauna and jacuzzi - no swimming pool or beauty treatments - just a caring atmosphere where a range of holistic therapies promote the process of self healing.

Proprietors Jo and Gerry Harvey have successfully created a homely and peaceful oasis, away from the pressures of modern life. Stress, they believe, to be a main cause of the body becoming out of balance, along with nutritionally depleted foods, lack of exercise and pollution. This philosophy is enhanced by a strict 'no smoking anywhere' policy and the absence of external influences such as newspapers, radios and television - even use of the telephone is discouraged.

Accommodation is in pleasant bedrooms, including some four poster rooms, each one decorated in a different shade and furnished with natural wood furniture and floral prints. Most of the bedrooms have wash-hand basins - but not en suite facilities.

Delicious, vegetarian wholefood cuisine is one of many pleasures of a stay at Middle Piccadilly - homegrown organic produce in season is used whenever possible.

Meals are taken very informally - like visiting family or friends and some help with the washing up is appreciated. There is a cosy lounge with open fire to relax beside and the picturesque Dorset countryside and coast to be explored.

Treatments

Remedial yoga, massage, aromatherapy and Neydharting moor baths complement a wide range of alternative health treatments here. These include acupressure, Bach flower remedies, counselling and regression therapy, creative visualisation, dietary therapy (with food allergy testing if necessary), reflexology, energy balancing, the Metamorphic Technique and alignment therapy.

Each guest's life pattern is investigated and advice given on the most appropriate treatment plan. Sometimes a combination of therapies may be prescribed, with a series of treatments given at progressively less intervals, to help retrain the body into a healthier way of life.

Tariff

The basic price per person per week is £305 or £45 per night, with treatments charged at £18.50 per hour.

A three-day holistic healing break is available for £230 per person inclusive of accommodation, meals, diagnostic session, sauna or jacuzzi, Neydharting moor bath and four treatments.

Travel Directions

Take motorway network and A30 to Sherborne, then A3030 road to Bishops Caundle and Holwell.

Nearest railway station Sherborne 4 miles.

NUTFIELD PRIORY
SURREY

ENGLAND southern

Nutfield Priory
Nutfield Redhill Surrey RH1 4EN
☏ 0737 822066   (Fx) 0737 823321

Price category C   A Hidden Hotel

Nutfield Priory was built in 1872 as an extravagant folly. Restored and refurbished in 1988, the elaborate carvings, cloisters, towers, stained glass windows and antiques create an unusual and comfortable country house hotel of great character.

Situated high on the Nutfield Ridge in 40 acres of grounds and enjoying far reaching views over the Surrey and Sussex countryside, Nutfield Priory is just seven miles from Gatwick airport with easy access to the M25.

All bedrooms are comfortably furnished and spacious with en suite bathrooms - some have jacuzzi bath. Thoughtful extras provided include fresh flowers, fruit and mineral water.

Dining in the unique cloistered restaurant is a novel and pleasant experience, as is relaxing in the elegant lounges cosy with blazing fires, or browsing among the books in the antique filled library.

Within the grounds is Fredericks, the extensive sports and leisure complex with a beautiful indoor pool, spa bath, steam room, sauna and two solaria with en suite showers. Sports amenities include fully equipped gymnasium, badminton court, three squash courts and snooker tables.

A comfortable lounge area with bar and restaurant is also within the complex, as well as a well-supervised crèche.

Admission to the pool and gymnasium is free, but steam, sauna, spa bath, solaria and sports facilities are charged extra, around £2.50 per session.

Treatments

Body treatments:

Aromatherapy and reflexology treatments are offered by a fully qualified therapist who is willing to provide a preliminary consultation and advice as part of a first appointment. Aromatherapy takes an hour and costs £20, reflexology 45 minute treatment £15, combined aromatherapy and reflexology £25.

Other treatments include G5 massage £9.50 or 10 sessions £80; back massage men and women £10.50; body massage for women £20; Folie Douce (steam bath, deep cleansing facial, back massage and manicure) £35.

Beauty treatments:

The wide range includes teenage facial £12; regular facials from £16; facial and make-up £32; waxing from £4.50; manicures and pedicures £7.50 to £11.75.

Tariff

Short breaks for two persons for two nights cost £256.25 and include accommodation, table d'hôte dinner, full cooked or continental breakfast, daily newspaper and temporary membership of the leisure club.

The regular tariff includes continental breakfast only (full breakfast £5.25 supplement) and costs from £80 single or £103 double room for two persons. Table d'hôte dinner costs around £19.95.

Travel Directions

M25 to junction 6, A25 to Redhill; or M25 to junction 8 and A25 through Redhill towards Godstone. Nutfield Priory is about 10 minutes' drive from both junctions and close to village of Nutfield.

Nearest railway station Redhill 1 1/2 miles.

PONTLANDS PARK
ESSEX

ENGLAND southern

Pontlands Park
West Hanningfield Rd Great Baddow Nr Chelmsford Essex CM2 8HR
☏ 0245 76444   (Fx) 0245 995411

| 17 |

Price category D

Pontlands Park originated in the mid-16th century, but was demolished when the present property was built in 1879. Converted into a country house hotel in 1981 by the Bartella family, it now boasts a fine new wing and state of the art health club and has won various prestigious awards for its excellence.

The hotel's health and leisure club is managed by Jenny Instrall, and has a wide range of body, beauty and health treatments which can be reserved in advance.

Leisure amenities in the health club include heated indoor and outdoor swimming pools, indoor and outdoor jacuzzis, sunbeds £3 or £6 per session, sauna and garden coffee shop.

Bedrooms at Pontlands Park (all named after flowers) are fully appointed with en suite bathroom, television, trouser press and hair drier. Four poster rooms available on request.

Treatments

Body treatments:

Vibrosaun (sauna, massage and soft music) 25 mins £7; Swedish full body massage £18; leg massage £8; back and neck massage £10; Decleor aroma massage £20; Vital Harmony body exfoliant with specific aromatherapy oils £20; Affinoderm slimming and remedial treatment £20; Aromatherm - to firm and improve poor circulation and muscular aches £20.

All Decleor body treatments include diagnostic massage followed by thermal blanket, and complimentary consultations are offered so guests can select the most suitable individual treatments.

Latest innovation in the beauty salon is the acquisition of Figure Shapers professional toning tables, six isometric machines providing an hour's pleasurable workout to tone the body.

Beauty treatments:

Decleor facials £20 each or course of 6 for £100; Seborreor facial £23; Hollywood facial £30; cleanse and make-up £10; eyelash tinting £6; manicure from £8; pedicure from £9; waxing from £3.75; electrolysis from £4.35.

A special thread vein treatment to remove broken or dilated capillaries costs £25.

Trimmers has an excellent hairdressing salon, offering a full range of services - cut and blow dry from £12; blow dry/shampoo and set from £7; cut and blow dry for men £8.50.

Tariff

Special two night weekend breaks inclusive of breakfast and use of leisure facilities £90 per person.

Regular nightly tariff from £66 to £77 single room, £75 to £96 double room.

These rates are for room only - breakfast if taken is from £4.50 - £8 per person.

All prices quoted are inclusive of VAT but do not include 10% service charge.

Travel Directions

A12 (Chelmsford By Pass) to Great Baddow Intersection (A130). Take first left slip road off A130 and keep left for Great Baddow, taking first left into West Hanningfield Road.

Nearest railway station Chelmsford approximately 4 miles.

THE SAWYERS
KENT

**ENGLAND
southern**

The Sawyers
High Street Hawkhurst Kent TN18 4PS
☎ 0580 754121   Fx 0580 754014

| 6 |

Price category C✵

This pretty little health farm retreat opened in 1991 and operates under the supervision of owner Maureen Jackson.

Set in a delightfully spacious 16th century country house, it is ideally situated on the Kent/Sussex borders amidst vineyards and orchards, and within walking distance of the Bedgebury Forest.

The Sawyers combines homely comforts like cosy lounges with log fires and inglenook fireplaces with modern exercise and treatment facilities. Amenities include steam cubicles and steam room, hydro spa baths, small heated outdoor pool (summer only), small gym, step-exerciser, sunbed and mountain bikes.

Tennis, squash, windsurfing, fishing, golf, visits to local vineyards, sightseeing and even hot-air ballooning are all available locally. Personal one-to-one fitness training can also be arranged.

Bedrooms are attractively furnished with lots of chintz and exposed beams. One room has en suite facilities including spa bath, other rooms share several luxurious bathrooms. Bathrobes and quality toiletries are provided for all visitors.

Meals are served in the pleasant dining room with the emphasis on healthy eating with low fat menus, fresh vegetables and fruit. Guests wanting to lose weight will be encouraged to do so, although fasting and starvation diets are not recommended. Sawyers aims to look after the individual needs of each guest, with amenities chosen via a questionnaire completed prior to arrival.

Treatments

A range of body, beauty and alternative health treatments are carried out by experienced practitioners and include aromatherapy, reflexology, hypnotherapy, psychology and astrology.

Tariff

A three-night break with all meals costs £199 per person - this price includes treatment consultation and two body massages.

The Sawyers is also open to non-residential guests for full day programmes which cost £55 and include:

Consultation with nutritionist on arrival, refreshment, hydro spa bath or steam, relaxation, lunch, relaxation (or treatment if required), sunbed, afternoon tea and departure.

Extra treatments such as reflexology, massage and facials can be booked in advance.

Travel Directions

Take M25 and exit at junction 5, taking A21 and then A268. Hawkhurst is 3 miles from junction of A21 and A268.

Nearest railway station Tunbridge Wells approximately 12 miles.

SELSDON PARK HOTEL
SURREY

ENGLAND southern

Selsdon Park Hotel
Sanderstead   South Croydon   Surrey   CR2 8YA
☏ 081-657 8811   (Fx) 081-651 6171

Price category B

This is a friendly and luxurious hotel with first class amenities set amid 200 acres of parkland in the Surrey countryside. Privately owned by the Sanderson family for many years, it is an ideal choice for a short healthy break.

In addition to the delightful Tropical Leisure Complex, the outdoor sports facilities are outstanding: 18-hole championship golf course, 9-hole putting green, driving range, heated outdoor pool, croquet lawn, boules pitch, jogging trail and four tennis courts - two floodlit, two grass. Indoors is a billiard room with four full-sized tables.

The Tropical Leisure Complex has a leisure pool, sauna, steam room, jacuzzi and sunbeds, as well as a gym, squash courts and poolside bar. Sunbeds and floodlit tennis courts have nominal charges.

All bedrooms are decorated and furnished to a high standard and have en suite bathroom and television, hair drier, trouser press, room bar and tea/coffee making facilities.

Stained-glass windows in the halls and stairways, polished wooden panelling and log fires all reflect the hotel's country house ambience.

Children are welcome and have their own play area. Baby sitting can be arranged in advance.

In the dining room there is an excellent choice of à la carte and table d'hôte menus, and a weekly dinner dance is held on Saturday evenings.

Treatments

Body treatments:

Aromatherapy £28; reflexology £20; Slendertone £8.50 or 6 for £45; Clarins body massage £20; back massage £15; back cleanse with muscle manipulation and infra-red treatment £18.50.

Beauty treatments:

Clarins Top to Toe treatment £52 (includes cleansing facial, soothing massage, manicure and pedicure); facials from £15; eyelash/brow tinting/shaping from £7.50; Clarins nail treatments from £13; ear piercing including 9ct gold ear studs and after-care treatment £12.50.

Tariff

Weekend breaks include accommodation, dinner on Friday, breakfast Saturday, Saturday dinner dance, Sunday breakfast - with full use of the amenities and one round of golf.

£170 to £198 per person sharing twin or double room.

Children have a discount up to 40 per cent on weekend breaks with parents, and special family tariffs are available in July and August.

Bargain low price winter packages are usually offered. The two night stay includes all meals and dinner dance, with special fitness programme arranged to include morning jogging, aerobics classes, tennis, squash and table tennis competitions, and a chance to play 18-holes of championship golf. Tariff on application.

Travel Directions

From central London take A23 Brighton road to Purley, then A22 Eastbourne road, and finally Downs Court Road for 2 1/2 miles. Hotel is 1/2 mile from the roundabout.

From other parts of the country Selsdon Park can be reached via M25, exit at junction 6 and then A22 to Whyteleafe. Turn right onto B270 then first left onto B269 Limpsfield Road. At roundabout take third exit onto A2022 to Selsdon.

Nearest railway station East Croydon approximately 3 miles and 10 minutes by taxi.

SOPWELL HOUSE
HERTFORDSHIRE

ENGLAND southern

Sopwell House
Cottonmill Lane   Sopwell   St Albans   Hertfordshire   AL1 2HQ
☏ 0727 864477   (Fx) 0727 44741

Price category C

Former home of the Mountbatten family, Sopwell House is now an elegant and peaceful country house hotel. Situated in 11 acres of landscaped gardens and grounds overlooking a golf course and the pleasant Hertfordshire countryside, the hotel is a few minutes' drive from four major motorways and just half an hour by road from central London.

An extensive refurbishment has further enhanced Sopwell House's country-style ambience - relaxing lounges with leather furniture and richly coloured drapes, and bedrooms offering every modern luxury and comfort while retaining the charm of a previous age.

Bedrooms are designed in country house style, with lavish furnishings, luxurious bathroom, telephone, hair drier, trouser press, satellite television, and tea/coffee making facilities.

Meals can be taken in the Magnolia Conservatory Restaurant, where diners enjoy imaginative cuisine served in the unusual setting of mature magnolia trees - the pink linen of the table cloths subtly echoing the floral theme.

Leisure amenities have been transformed with the recent opening of a superb new Country Club and Spa, offering hotel residents and private members facilities and services surpassing those found at many health farms. The Country Club's philosophy is to promote an improved quality of life using exercise, diet and relaxation holistically.

The outstanding facilities include a large ozone treated pool, spa bath, sauna, steam room, relaxation area and sun terrace, solaria, supervised health and fitness suite with the latest high tech equipment and personal programmes, beauty suite with four treatment rooms, hairdressing, poolside cafe and snooker room.

The Brasserie overlooks the pool and gardens and serves informal healthy meals and snacks, catering for those on reduced diets or seeking vegetarian menus.

Treatments

Body treatments:

Full Decleor range with an initial diagnostic massage followed by a thermal body wrap - Vital Harmony £25; Affinoderm £25; bust care treatment £20.

Thalgo balneotherapy using deep massage spa baths, full body scrub and application of gel containing micronised sea algae and essential oils. Thalgo silhouette toning and refining treatment £25; cellulite treatment £25; relaxation and moisturising £25. Thalgo wraps and hydrotherapy £25 per treatment.

G5 massage £14; underwater massage £14; spa massage bath £14; Slendertone £11.50 per session or 6 for £42.

Beauty treatments:

Decleor range facials from £23; make-up £12; superfirming pre-make-up facial £18; waxing from £6.50; eyebrow and eyelash tint £9; ladies manicure £8; gents manicure £7; pedicure £9.

The club also has its own hairdressing salon with a full complement of services.

Half day and full day *Top to Toe* programmes incorporating use of the facilities and a range of treatments are available from £45.

Tariff

Two night *Getaway* breaks cost £75 per person Monday to Thursday or £60 per person Friday to Sunday. This rate includes accommodation in twin/double room, breakfast, three course dinner or à la carte allowance each day.

Two night *Romantic* breaks cost £175 per person and include pink champagne, smoked salmon sandwiches and flowers on arrival. Accommodation in four poster room, candlelit dinner, traditional breakfast, souvenir bathrobe.

Regular nightly tariff for room only is £89.75 mid-week and £64.75 weekends single, or £99.75 mid-week and £74.75 weekends double room (accommodating two persons).

Light breakfast is £5.50 and full English breakfast £7.50. All hotel residents have use of new leisure facilities during their stay.

Travel Directions

Easily accessible from M1, M10, M25 and A1(M), take A1081 or A414 Hatfield to St Albans road.

Nearest railway station St Albans approximately 2 miles.

ENGLAND
southern

SPA HOTEL
KENT

The Spa Hotel
Mount Ephraim Tunbridge Wells Kent TN4 8XJ
ⓒ 0892 520331   Fx 0892 510575

| 75 |

Price category C

Situated in the elegant spa town of Tunbridge Wells, the Spa Hotel was originally built as a country mansion in 1766. An hotel for over a century, it enjoys an ideal setting amid parkland, landscapes and lakes.

All bedrooms are individually designed with en suite bathroom, television, hair drier, telephone and tea/coffee making facilities.

The hotel's public rooms are spacious and comfortable; coffee and afternoon tea can be taken in the lounge or residents can browse in the Victorian library.

Pre-dinner drinks and snacks are provided in the Equestrian bar, and the grand Regency restaurant features imaginative menus created with fresh produce from Kentish farms and the London markets.

The Sparkling Health leisure centre in the hotel overlooks the gardens and has a wide choice of health, leisure and sporting amenities including indoor swimming pool, spa pool, saunas, sunbeds, gym with the latest apparatus, mirrored exercise room, beauty therapy clinic, hairdressing salon, floodlit tennis court, fitness trail, children's adventure playground and games room.

Treatments

Although most sporting facilities are free to hotel residents, all treatments at the Pinx beauty clinic are charged extra.

Body treatments:

Full body massage £21; back massage with infra red £12; aromatherapy £28 for first treatment then £25 subsequently or 6 for £120; body paraffin wax £24 each, 6 for £120; reflexology £18; G5 massage from £10 per session, 6 for £52; Slendertone from £9 per session, 6 for £48; mixed course 6 x G5 and faradic treatments used together £63; seaweed cold wrap £18.50; body contouring treatment £25; waxing from £4.50; electrolysis from £4.

Pinx Pamper Parcel costs £25 and includes sauna, body exfoliation with salt rub and massage with essential oils, relaxation and herbal tea.

Beauty treatments:

Facials include Cathiodermie £21; Geloide Prescription £17; Thalgo with collagen £28; basic facial £15; basic facial with steam £17; aromatherapy facial £18.

Cleanse and make-up £10; collagen eye treatment £20; eye contour treatment £16.50; eyelash tinting £6; manicure and massage £7.50; pedicure and massage £9.50.

Top to Toe package including lunch, tea and coffee - 4 1/2 hours - £55; with blow dry £63.50; with cut and blow dry £71.50.

The beauty salon is closed on Sundays but all other facilities in Sparkling Health are available.

Tariff

Bargain two night breaks including dinner, bed and breakfast cost £59 per person nightly sharing a standard room, or £66 in a four poster or de luxe room.

Two children under 16 sharing parents' accommodation stay free of charge with meals charged for as taken.

Regular nightly tariff for accommodation only - from £69 single, £84 double room. Full English breakfast £7.50.

Travel Directions

Mount Ephraim is to the north of the town centre of Tunbridge Wells.
Nearest railway station Tunbridge Wells Central less than a mile.

ENGLAND southern

TYRINGHAM CLINIC
BUCKINGHAMSHIRE

Tyringham Naturopathic Clinic
Newport Pagnell   Buckinghamshire   MK16 9ER
✆   0908 610450

Price category E✻

Tyringham, the UK's largest residential naturopathic clinic, is situated in a pleasantly secluded part of rural Buckinghamshire, and offers a comprehensive range of naturopathic treatments and therapies.

The sandstone Georgian mansion is set amid 30 acres of gardens, woodlands and farmlands, and is easily reached just two miles from Newport Pagnell.

This is not a beauty orientated health farm - visitors expecting facials and slimming treatments will be disappointed by the absence of such amenities. Tyringham is a place to come to re-educate lifestyle habits and cultivate a more natural approach to health.

Guests are accepted for a minimum stay of a week, with three weeks recommended for maximum benefit.

Wholesome vegetarian fare is served in a somewhat austere dining room reminiscent of a school refectory - basic cutlery, glasses and condiments on the tables, no flowers or table cloths to brighten up mealtimes. Menus are compiled for variety and nutritional value - special diets are prescribed when necessary.

Therapeutic fasting can also be carried out, with carefully monitored low intakes of food and drink. Some inflexibility has been shown in the serving of these special diets, so potential guests are advised to insist on getting the correct individual choice of food. No coffee or tea is served at Tyringham - only herbal teas or mineral water.

No smoking is the rule in all public rooms - smokers can retire to the smokers' lounge if the urge to have a cigarette becomes unbearable.

There are many leisure facilities to be enjoyed - badminton, tennis, croquet, putting, crazy golf, table tennis and a variety of card and board games. Tyringham boasts Europe's largest private outdoor pool which although unheated, is enjoyed by many hardy individuals in the summer months.

Treatments

Visitors suffering from a variety of complaints are accepted and treated with a broad spectrum of alternative treatments - specific therapies are selected to meet individual needs.

Therapies used include acupuncture, physiotherapy, osteopathy and stress release. Qualified practitioners supervise all treatments, and qualified nurses are on call at all times.

Tyringham specialises in hydrotherapy, with sitz baths, Scottish douche, salt water and mineral baths available. A heated therapeutic pool is used for exercise in conjunction with a jacuzzi and sauna.

Tariff

Tyringham is a registered charity and as such is non-profit making. Charges made cover administration and running costs only, and in cases of need, generous reductions can be made through the Needy Patient's Fund. This applies only to dormitory accommodation, which costs from £210 per person per week, depending on the season.

Other accommodation is in single and double rooms, the majority having en suite facilities and charges range from £250 to £377 per person for twin-bedded accommodation. Single rooms cost from £349 to £465 per week.

The weekly tariff includes consultations and treatments as prescribed - separate charges are made for X-rays, blood tests, ECGs, injections and medications.

Although all stays at Tyringham are for a week's duration, outpatients can enjoy a Tyringham day, staying at the Swan Revived Hotel, in the charming town of Newport Pagnell.

Accommodation, English breakfast, lunch at Tyringham, and a full day's health programme and dinner costs £54 per person - bookings to be made via Tyringham.

Staff at Tyringham are friendly and helpful, and the atmosphere is much less formal than the brochure suggests.

Travel Directions

From M1 exit at junction 14 and take A509 to Newport Pagnell and B526 to Tyringham.

Nearest railway stations Wolverton 5 miles, Milton Keynes 8 miles.

VERDE
DORSET

**ENGLAND
southern**

Verde
167 Seabourne Road   Southbourne   Bournemouth   Dorset   BH5 2HH
✆   0202 428404

Price category D✲

Verde Bodycare Holidays are unique, offering an intensive week of health, beauty and fitness treatments at the Verde Studios in Southbourne, a suburb of Bournemouth. Here you can learn to keep healthy and trim with dietary counselling, aromatherapy remedial massage and fitness lessons.

All visitors have an initial consultation with Verde's owner, Mrs Annabelle Lazenby, to plan a personalised schedule of treatments and counselling for the forthcoming week. Accommodation is arranged at Mrs Lazenby's hotel, St Wilfred's, a short walk away, allowing visitors to enjoy a range of optional health and body treatments at very reasonable prices in this busy salon, situated on the main Seabourne Road.

St Wilfred's twin-bedded rooms have shared bathroom facilities, including a spa bath. All food is carefully chosen for its nutritional content. Breakfast and dinner are served at the hotel, and a low fat nutritious lunch at Verde Studios. On Sundays, only breakfast and dinner are served, as most visitors arrive, depart or go sightseeing on this day of the week.

Treatments
Body treatments:
Daily fitness lessons £2; thalassotherapy £6.78; hydrotherapy bath £4.95; remedial massage £14.50; G5 massage with slenderising gel £8.95; waxing from £2.98.

Beauty treatments:
Colour analysis with make-up lessons and personal grooming arranged by appointment £30; facials from £6.95; manicure £4.95; pedicure £4.95; eyebrow/eyelash tinting £5.

Skin care is based on French seaweed products known for their anti-ageing properties.

Hairdressing and hair care treatments are also available using natural ingredients such as juniper, burdock and sesame.

Tariff
The daily tariff per person sharing a twin-bedded room from May to September is £45, £230 weekly or £330 for ten days. From September to May the rates are slightly less at £40 per day, £195 per week or £295 for ten days. These prices include counselling (optional treatments extra) and all meals except lunch on Sunday.

New for 1992 are the *Therapy for Life* courses which cost £285 per person and include all meals (except Sunday lunch) and accommodation, various treatments of choice, dietary advice, fitness lessons and aromatherapy remedial massage.

Travel Directions
Verde Bodycare Holidays are situated in Bournemouth close to the beaches and within walking distance of the shopping centre.

Nearest railway station Bournemouth approximately 2 miles.

ENGLAND
south west

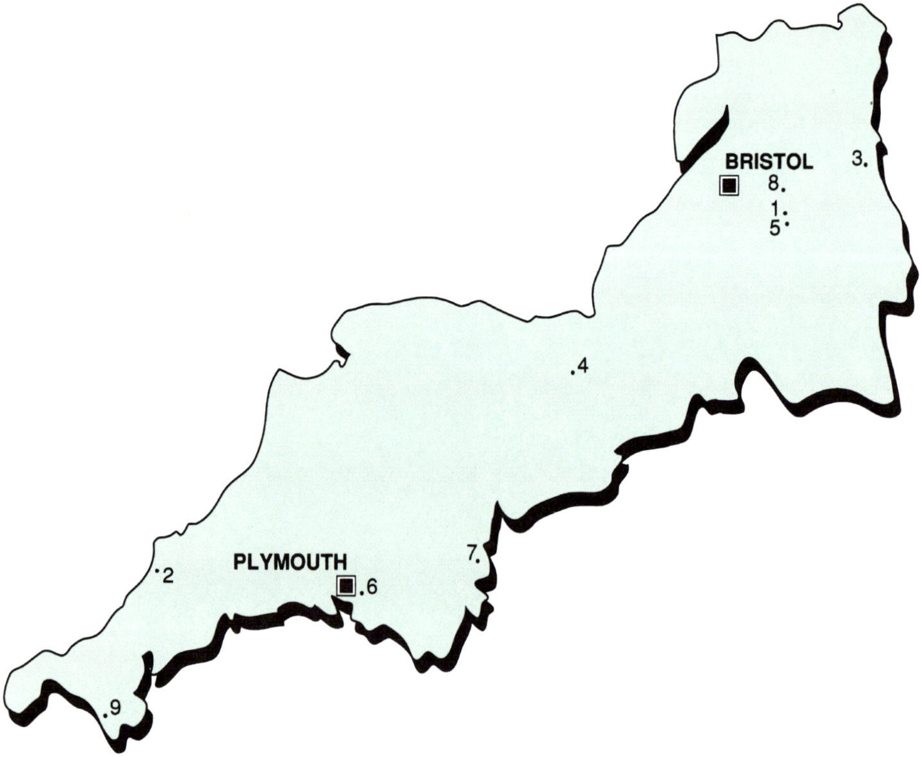

ESTABLISHMENTS IN SOUTH WEST ENGLAND

Map ref.		Page no.
1	Bath Spa Hotel	90
2	Bedruthan Steps	92
3	Blunsdon House	95
4	Cedar Falls	97
5	Combe Grove Manor	100
6	Elfordleigh	103
7	Lorrens	105
8	Lucknam Park	108
9	Polurrian Hotel	110

ENGLAND south west

BATH SPA HOTEL
AVON

Bath Spa Hotel
Sydney Road   Bath   Avon   BA2 6JF
(℃)   0225 444424   (Fx)   0225 444006

Price category A   A Forte Exclusive Hotel

The Bath Spa Hotel is situated amidst acres of landscaped gardens overlooking the city, a ten minute walk away.

The 19th century mansion has now re-opened after a mammoth renovation, restoring its former glory as a luxury hotel in the grandest tradition.

The architectural features of the building have been enhanced by rich furnishings and tasteful decor, and all main lounges retain the atmosphere and refinement of a previous era. Traditional afternoon tea is taken in the Colonnade overlooking the gardens, or beside the fire on colder days.

The luxurious bedrooms have en suite bathroom, telephone, satellite television, mini-bar and 24 hour room service.

International cuisine of high standard with table d'hôte and à la carte menus is served in the gracious Vellore restaurant, designed in classic style with Roman columns and chandeliers.

As befits a premier hotel in a city that was once England's leading spa, there is a well equipped health and leisure facility for use by hotel guests, but unfortunately no spa water is used in treatments or bathing. The Laurels has a large heated indoor swimming pool, jacuzzi, two saunas, fully equipped gym with instruction and personal assessment availability, outdoor tennis court and croquet lawn.

Treatments

Body treatments:

Hotel beautician Michelle offers a comprehensive range of body treatments in the Beauty Salon including:

Full body massage £25; aromatherapy £35; back, neck and shoulder massage £15; quick-slim body wrap £25; Slendertone treatment £10; G5 massage £10; waxing from £5; electrolysis from £6.50; red vein treatment £20.

Beauty treatments:

A varied range of facials for all skin types and ages is available, using French GM Collin professional products and these cost from £20. Other beauty treatments include cleanse and make-up £15; colour analysis and make-up £25; eyelash tint £6.95.

Tariff

The Bath Spa holds special interest weekends throughout the year and a recent innovation has been the *De-stress weekend* which costs £370 per person (additional treatments £30 per hour).

These include individual sessions with a psychotherapist with techniques to reduce tension, a fitness assessment and work-out programme, aromatherapy or shiatsu massage, special light and healthy menus.

Weekend leisure breaks are available for two to four nights (must include a Saturday night) from £105 per person per night, and are inclusive of accommodation, table d'hôte dinner in the Vellore restaurant and full English breakfast.

The regular tariff is presently £110 single room, £140 double room and £170 four poster room. These rates include service and VAT but not breakfast.

Travel Directions

From M4 - exit at junction 18 taking A46 to Bath approximately 8 miles, following signs for city centre.

Nearest railway station Bath approximately 1 mile.

ENGLAND south west

BEDRUTHAN STEPS HOTEL
CORNWALL

Bedruthan Steps Hotel
Mawgan Porth   Cornwall   TR8 4BU
☏ 0637 860555   Fx 0637 860714

100

Price category E/D

This modern and friendly resort hotel is situated in five acres of grounds overlooking the spectacular coastline of North Cornwall. A golden sandy beach lies below the hotel, which takes its name from the National Trust beauty spot Bedruthan Steps, a short walk away.

Bedruthan Steps is ideal for happy family holidays, as children are made especially welcome with their own dining room, en suite bedrooms, indoor and outdoor swimming pools, sports facilities and tournaments. There is also an adventure playground, cinema, sandpits, holiday clubs and special activities organised during the holiday season. A special nanny service is available at the reasonable charge of £2 per hour per child. Baby sitting can be arranged and all rooms have baby alarms.

These thoughtful arrangements leave parents free to enjoy the outstanding facilities of the hotel for themselves, in particular the splendid health and fitness amenities.

These include indoor and outdoor pools, hydro spa and plunge pool, saunas, solaria, and steam cabinets.

Sporting facilities are free of charge and include tennis, squash, racquet ball, table tennis and full sized snooker and pool tables. Sports tournaments, football, rounders and netball matches are regularly organised for all age groups. It is planned to start some exercise and aerobics classes in the near future.

Accommodation is on a half board basis, and includes continental breakfast, three course dinner with coffee (or buffet lunch if preferred). Full board terms are £4 extra per person daily, and packed lunches can be made up instead of lunch.

All bedrooms have en suite facilities, television, fridge, tea/coffee making facilities and baby-listening devices.

A variety accommodation is available - small rooms with a rear view, villa suites in a separate building linked to the main hotel by a gallery, and de luxe apartment suites complete with four poster bed and bathroom with jacuzzi. There are also a few single rooms with country views.

The Cornish cuisine is particularly good, as the hotel produces its own smoked ham, beef and chicken as well as organic vegetables and fruit grown in its own gardens. Bread and croissants are baked daily and there is always a vegetarian choice on the extensive mouth-watering menu. Special diets (diabetic, gluten free etc) can be catered for with advanced notice.

Treatments

Body treatments:

Aromatherapy massage treatment with hot oils £15 or £18 with infra red heat; cellulite seaweed massage £20; G5 massage £8 per session; aromatherapy steam cabinet £10; reflexology £15, etc.

Beauty treatments:

Waxing from £1.75; eyelash tinting £4; manicure with polish £6.50, with paraffin wax treatment £11.50; pedicure with polish £7, with paraffin wax treatment £12; hot paraffin wax treatment for arthritic hands £5.

Beauty treatments for the face include aromatherapy facial £16; facial and make-up lesson £14; steam facial £10; basic facial (cleanse, mask, tone and moisturise) £9.50; paraffin wax facial £18.

A full range of hairdressing services including perms, tints and highlights is available in the hair salon.

Nutritional therapy and the Alexander Technique can also be given within the health and beauty complex by special arrangement.

Tariff

Bedruthan Steps Hotel is open from the beginning of April until October each year and features a variety of short break holidays including health and beauty breaks.

Prices start at £24 daily per person for a rear view room in low season or £29 per person for a seaview suite. Treatments are planned individually and charged extra.

This incredibly low price includes breakfast and dinner with coffee.

Prices for a one week (seven night) holiday vary from £178 - £221 per person in the low season to £300 - £321 per person in the peak July/August period. This is inclusive of accommodation and half board for seven nights, with full use of all sporting and leisure amenities.

Altogether a super resort hotel for all the family with wonderful views and excellent facilities at reasonable rates.

Travel Directions

Via motorway network signed towards North Cornwall and Newquay. Mawgan Porth is on B3276, off the main A30 Bodmin to Penzance road, a few miles north of Newquay.

Nearest railway station Newquay approximately 6 miles.

BLUNSDON HOUSE HOTEL
WILTSHIRE

ENGLAND south west

Blunsdon House Hotel
Blunsdon Swindon Wiltshire SN2 4AD
☏ 0793 721701   (Fx) 0793 721056

Price category C

Blunsdon House Hotel is situated two miles north of Swindon in spacious private grounds of 70 acres. Originally a farm guest house, Blunsdon House has grown in size and status over the years, and is now one of Wiltshire's leading country house hotels.

The Clifford family have created a fine and comfortable establishment with excellent features and facilities, including a new £1.2 million leisure club. All hotel residents can use the amenities - swimming pool, spa bath, toddlers' splash pool, saunas, steam rooms, sunbeds, and supervised well-equipped gym.

Sports facilities available include squash courts, snooker tables, skittles, darts, 'artificial' grass tennis court, one mile woodland walk/

jogging track, and rooms with computer games. There is also a supervised crèche.

All rooms at Blunsdon House have en suite facilities and are spacious and comfortable. There is no extra charge for children sharing parents' room and meals are charged for as taken. Reception can 'baby listen' during the evenings for parents in the hotel. Baby-sitting can be arranged if prior notice is given. Ground floor accommodation, four poster rooms and 'Prestige' rooms with spa bath are available on request.

There is a choice of three bars and two restaurants within the hotel. The Ridge Restaurant with à la carte and fixed price English and continental cuisine, and Carrie's Carverie with a selection of table d'hôte dishes in a more informal setting.

Treatments

In the Beauty Therapy Room a wide range of body and beauty treatments are carried out by two qualified therapists who are happy to offer free consultations without obligation.

Body treatments:

Elemis aromatic body massage with body brushing to stimulate the circulation and improve texture and tone £20; 45 minute body massage £13; 20 minute back massage £7; ozone back scrub with skin peel and clay mask £10.50; 15 minute Niagara treatment on vibrating therapy table to help alleviate aches and pains, tension and exhaustion £5.

Beauty treatments:

Facials from £8.50 - £20; manicure £6.95; pedicure £8.50; eye treatments from £3.50; waxing and epilation £3.50 to £12.

Special *Executive Lady* afternoons from 1 - 6 pm cost £45 and are inclusive of use of Leisure Club facilities with optional physiological assessment (resting heart rate, blood pressure and body composition analysis), Elemis body massage or Elemis facial, Niagara treatments, and sunbed. Hairdressing appointments can also be arranged.

Tariff

Getaway weekends are available from £59 per person per night inclusive of accommodation, breakfast and dinner on Friday and Saturdays, with a reduced half board charge of £28.50 per person when Sunday is taken as a third night.

Standard accommodation charges for bed and breakfast start at £69.50 single and £92.50 for a double/twin room. The standard prices include VAT but not service charge.

Travel Directions

From M4 exit at junction 15, then take A419 dual carriageway to Cirencester for 7 miles, turning right at sign to Broad Blunsdon.

Nearest railway station Swindon 2 miles.

CEDAR FALLS
SOMERSET

ENGLAND south west

Cedar Falls Health Farm
Bishops Lydeard Taunton Somerset TA4 3HR
☏ 0823 433233 & 0823 433338 (reservations) (Fx) 0823 432777

| 33 |

Price category B✲

Cedar Falls is situated on the outskirts of the little Somerset village of Bishops Lydeard, close to Exmoor National Park. The red stone mansion house is set in a 40 acre estate with landscaped gardens, lakes and woods, and offers a wide range of health, beauty and sports amenities.

The accent is very much on relaxation. Staff are friendly and helpful and although there are many exercise classes and activities, visitors can be as active or as lazy as they choose. Stress management talks with counselling sessions and workshops are popular innovations.

Everyone has an initial consultation on arrival when dietary goals are discussed. Guests can seek the advice of a nutritional adviser each morning if they need help in planning the day's dietary requirements.

Two pleasant dining rooms cater for most types of diet, with the emphasis on raw and natural foods. Salad lunches are taken buffet-style, with a choice of main courses for the evening meal. Food is satisfying and plentiful with delicious home-baked bread.

Guests have unlimited use of the sports facilities which include outdoor badminton, swimming pools (indoor and outdoor), tennis, trim-track, croquet, putting, fly-fishing in the trout-stocked lake and 18-hole par 3 golf course. Indoor amenities include heated indoor swimming pool, sauna, jacuzzi, steamroom, solarium and gym.

Exercise classes and aquarobics are held regularly, and alternative health treatments - acupuncture, iridology, osteopathy and reflexology can be arranged on request.

Talks on aspects of health, lifestyle and general interest topics feature regularly in the evenings, as well as beauty and cookery demonstrations.

The atmosphere at Cedar Falls is relaxed and informal at all times, with most guests opting to wear track suits or casual clothes during the day and slightly more formal wear for dinner. Casual and informal clothing and sportswear, books, toiletries and gifts can be purchased from the boutique.

Treatments

Additional beauty and slimming treatments should be reserved when confirming reservations.

Body treatments:

Ten types of massage ranging from a hand or foot massage £11 to £34.50 for a Paris Method body massage; aromatherapy £34.50; Slendertone £11.50 or 5 for £46; G5 massage £14.95; solarium £3.50; sauna £6.90; steam treatment £6.90; mud pack £6.90; Ionithermie £41.40; waxing from £4.60.

Beauty treatments:

Manicure £10.93; pedicure £16.10; eight different types of facials from £11.50 to £32.50.

Cedar Falls was the first health farm to use the exclusive Elemis range of natural beauty products, which are very luxurious and environmentally friendly. Elemis treatments start with a special introduction that includes body brushing, back massage and a personal consultation.

Tariff

The daily tariff includes accommodation, meals and three daily treatments (daily massage or G5, steam or sauna, aromatherapy, peat bath or solarium).

Following a recent refurbishment, all rooms now have en suite facilities, with six categories of accommodation starting from £75 per night per person single room or £68 per person sharing a double room to the most expensive rate of £139 single room or £125 per person sharing a double room.

Several non-residential day programmes are available with prices depending on treatment selection.

Top to Toe Day £51.75 (full body massage, sauna or steam, solarium, 1/2 hour facial)

Special Beauty Day £56.35 (1/2 hour facial, manicure, pedicure, make-up).

Elemis Aromatic Day £90 (1 hour facial, 1 1/2 hour aroma massage, steam, sauna or special bath, hair and scalp massage with blow dry, complimentary aromatherapy burner)

Clarins Special Day £71.30 (facial, body treatment including massage, manicure, pedicure).

Travel Directions

Leave M5 at junction 25 and take A358 to Minehead. Ignore right-hand signs into Bishops Lydeard and continue for 1/2 mile, turning right over a small bridge. Cedar Falls drive is immediately on the left.

Nearest railway station Taunton (5 miles).

ENGLAND south west

COMBE GROVE MANOR
AVON

Combe Grove Manor
Brassknocker Hill   Monkton Combe   Bath   Avon   BA2 7HS
☏ 0225 834644   Fx 0225 834961

Price category C

This gracious English manor house is situated on the hillside site of a Roman settlement, amid 68 acres of gardens and woodlands with extensive views over the Limpley Stoke valley. On a clear day the famous White Horse of Westbury is visible, 16 miles away.

The present owners purchased Combe Grove Manor in 1985 and have carefully preserved its unique 18th century elegance while renovating and transforming it into a luxurious hotel and country club with modern comforts and unrivalled sports, health and leisure facilities.

Accommodation is provided in either the Manor House itself or the charming Garden Lodge adjacent to the Country Club.

Bedrooms are individually designed in delightful country house style, with luxurious bathroom, bathrobes, satellite television, telephone and tea/coffee making facilities.

Interesting and substantial table d'hôte and à la carte menus are served in the elegant Restaurant with its lovely views across the wooded valley, or less formally in the Manor Vaults, which has a good choice of dishes and bar facilities.

The Country Club amenities include indoor and outdoor swimming pools, Nautilus gym with cardio-vascular equipment, aerobics studio with fully sprung wooden floor, hydro spa heated to 101°F, steam room, saunas, solarium and beauty salon.

Sporting facilities include one covered and four all-weather tennis courts, three squash courts, woodchip jogging trail through estate woodlands, 5-hole par 3 golf course, 9-hole mini putting course, 17-station two tiered driving range.

Hotel residents enjoy full use of these outstanding facilities, and can join in aerobic or fitness classes. Body and beauty treatments should be reserved in advance to avoid disappointment.

Treatments

Body treatments:

Full aromatherapy and reflexology (2 hours) £28; standard body massage £16; back massage £8; G5 massage £6, 8 for £42; Slendertone £8 per hour, 8 for £56; complete body firming treatment £17; bust treatment £11; waxing from £4.50.

Beauty treatments:

Clarins Deep Cleansing facial £16; Revitalising and Firming facial £17.50; Double Serum facial £45; make-up lesson £15; eyelash tinting £4.50; manicure £8; pedicure £10; electrolysis from £5.

Tariff

Ordinary weekend breaks cost from £130 per room (two persons) per night (minimum two nights stay) inclusive of continental breakfast and dinner in the Georgian Restaurant.

Two night *Health and Fitness* breaks incorporating a full programme of leisure activities and sports tuition cost £175 per room (two persons) per night and includes dinner and accommodation on the first evening, continental breakfast, lunch in the Manor Vaults, dinner and accommodation on day two, and a continental breakfast on the morning of departure.

Specialist calorie controlled menus available on request to meet individual requirements. A fully co-ordinated fitness programme is organised for the visit and includes tennis, squash, swimming and gym personal coaching. A body massage is also included in the break.

Clarins Top to Toe Breaks start at £140 per person per night (for single occupancy) or £105 per night per person sharing twin occupancy. The break includes Paris Method facial, a Paris Method body treatment, manicure and pedicure, continental breakfast and dinner in the Georgian Restaurant.

Standard hotel tariff starts at £100 for a standard double/twin room in the Garden Lodge or £110 for a standard double room in the Manor House. De luxe bedrooms, four poster rooms and suites are available at supplementary cost.

Travel Directions

Exit M4 at junction 18 and follow signs to Bath for 10 miles. Combe Grove Manor can be reached taking either the A3062 or the A36 from Bath city centre, approximately 2 miles.

Nearest railway station Bath approximately 2 miles.

ELFORDLEIGH
DEVON

ENGLAND south west

Elfordleigh Hotel and Country Club
Colebrook Plympton Devon PL7 5EB
☎ 0752 336428   (Fx) 0752 344581

| 20 |

Price category C

Elfordleigh Hotel and Country Club lies on the edge of Dartmoor in 65 acres of gardens, woodlands and manicured lawns, with extensive views over the lovely Plym Valley. Originally a major west country seat, this gracious hotel has recently been refurbished and extended by owners Robert and Tina Palace, to offer the visitor outstanding facilities and comfortable accommodation.

The hotel has 20 double rooms furnished in country house style, all with en suite bathroom, satellite television, telephone and tea/coffee making facilities. Downstairs are four comfortable lounges and several bars in which to unwind with a relaxing drink before dinner or after some energetic sporting activity.

The hotel has two restaurants serving à la carte and table d'hôte meals - the informal Country Pantry and the elegant Churchill's Restaurant complete with oak-panelled walls, conservatory and silver service. There is also a coffee shop serving light snacks throughout the day.

All hotel residents have full use of Elfordleigh's private country club, with its exceptional range of health and fitness facilities including a Roman style indoor heated pool with pine ceiling, jacuzzi, palm trees and separate refreshments area, sauna, solarium, steam room, fitness room/gym and jogging track.

Residents can also enjoy the many sporting facilities on offer including 18-hole par 68 golf course, golf practice area and putting green, outdoor heated pool with sunbathing patio, glass-backed squash court, three all-weather tennis courts with floodlights and tennis pavilion, croquet lawn, full sized snooker table, and games room complete with table tennis, darts and pool tables.

Treatments

The beauty room offers a range of body and facial treatments at competitive prices.

Body treatments:

Body massage £16; back massage £10; G5 massage £10; Slendertone £10; waxing £2 to £17, etc.

Beauty treatments:

Eyebrow and eyelash tinting £7 or £4 each; 45 minutes make-up £10; manicure £6.50; pedicure £7.50; basic facial using René Guinot products £15; Cathiodermie £20; Bio-Peel £12.

Tariff

A two night weekend break costs £118 per person and includes accommodation, dinner, bed and breakfast and full use of health and leisure facilities including free use of the golf course (to guests showing official handicap). Extra night (half board) either side of the weekend £50. Single supplement £10 per night.

Stays of four nights or more cost £50 per person per night for dinner/bed and breakfast.

Daily tariff for accommodation and full English breakfast £53.50 single, £89 twin or double and £96 family room.

Travel Directions

Take A374 Plympton road from Marsh Mills roundabout, turning left into Larkham Lane and into Crossway.

At Boringdon Hill, turn left and continue for a further mile.

Nearest railway station Plymouth 7 miles.

LORRENS
DEVON

ENGLAND south west

Lorrens Health Hydro
Cary Park   Babbacombe   Torquay   Devon   TQ1 3NN
✆ 0803 323740

Price category C✲

Pleasantly situated some 500 yards from Babbacombe Downs in lovely Devon, Lorrens Health Hydro is England's only coastal health farm. A health farm with a difference - it caters exclusively for ladies, with the emphasis on total relaxation and pampering in a stress-free environment.

Owned and managed personally by Valerie, Peter and Steve Vickerstaff with an enthusiastic and professional staff, Lorrens aims to provide the highest standards of personal attention at all times. The maximum number of guests accommodated at any one time is never more than 20.

Facilities have recently been extended and now include outdoor heated swimming pool and sun terrace (summer only), spa pool, steam room, sauna, fully equipped gym and exercise studio.

A computerised fitness assessment service is offered - this takes about an hour and analyses aerobic capacity, cardio-vascular fitness and body fat percentage. An ideal target weight is provided, taking into account age, body type and current weight. The appraisal is free to guests staying for ten days or more or £7.50 as an optional treatment.

All ladies have a consultation with a member of staff on their first day, when personal needs and dietary requirements are discussed and a suggested programme worked out.

A well-balanced de-toxification diet is provided, including fresh vegetables, fish and chicken dishes, salads and fresh fruit. Several vegetarian dishes are served every day.

All rooms are comfortably furnished and tastefully decorated, with matching toiletries and lots of large bath towels. Most rooms have en suite bathroom, all have television and tea/coffee making facilities.

Guests travelling long distances can extend their stay by arriving the evening before their first day of treatments.

These usually start after lunch on the first day.

Treatments

The number of treatments included in the tariff depends on the length of stay - the minimum package is the *5 Day Slimaway* (four nights) which includes instructed gym work-outs, 2 body massages, 3 x G5 massages, 5 Slendertone treatments, 2 vacuum suctions, 1 special Sixtus pedicure, full use of the spa pool, steam room and sauna throughout.

Body treatments:

Optional slimming and body treatments include full body massage £16; aromatherapy £20; G5 massage £10; Slendertone £10; vacuum suction £10 per treatment; sunbed £1.50; aerobic classes £2.50 or 5 for £10; waxing from £3; electrolysis from £5.

Beauty treatments:

Facials from £15; Cathiodermie facial masque and relaxing massage £20; Bio-Peel and Cathiodermie £30; eyelash or eyebrow tinting £4; make-up lesson with cleanse and tone £12; manicure £5.50; Sixtus pedicure £9.50.

Tariff

5 Day Slimaway (four nights) - single room with en suite facilities £280; single room without facilities £250.

7 Day Slimaway (six nights) - single room with en suite facilities £375.50; single room without facilities £330.

10 Day Slimaway (nine nights) single room with en suite facilities £530; single room without facilities £470.

14 Day Slimaway (13 nights) single room with en suite facilities £742; single room without facilities £658.

Two persons sharing a twin-bedded room receive 10% discount per person.

Please note - tariffs are EXCLUSIVE of VAT, which will be added at the current rate to all accounts.

Travel Directions

Take A374 Plympton road from Marsh Mills roundabout, turning left into Larkham Lane and into Crossway.

At Boringdon Hill, turn left and continue for a further mile.

Nearest railway station Plymouth 7 miles.

**ENGLAND
south west**

LUCKNAM PARK
WILTSHIRE

Lucknam Park
Colerne   Wiltshire   SN14 8AZ
☏   0225 742777   (Fx)   0225 743536

| 39 |

Price category B/A

Built in 1720 in countryside on the southern edge of the Cotswolds, Lucknam Park has been converted into an elegant hotel with first class health and leisure facilities.

An impressive mile-long avenue lined with beech trees leads up to the Georgian mansion, decorated and furnished in period style with an abundance of fresh flower arrangements. Housed within the walls of the old garden is the Leisure Spa with heated indoor swimming pool, whirlpool spa, steam room, sauna, gymnasium, solarium, beauty salon, hairdresser and snooker room.

Outdoor sporting enthusiasts will find floodlit tennis courts, a croquet lawn and many pleasant walks in the grounds. Other sporting activities such as golf, fishing, boating, horse riding and even hot air ballooning can be arranged.

Bedrooms are spacious with splendid views and beautiful furnishings, all have en suite bathroom, television and telephone.

The stylish restaurant offers good food and friendly service with a wide choice of modern English cuisine complemented by an excellent wine list.

Treatments

Body treatments:

Full body massage £25; aromatherapy £30; back and neck massage £14; full body massage by machine to boost lymph and blood circulation £20; Slendertone £40 for 5 treatments; solarium £5 per 1/2 hour.

Beauty treatments:

Facials (from £23) are especially good here - all include skin analysis, cleanse, tone and massage of face, neck and shoulders. This is followed by an application of a suitable mask and oils or moisturisers; manicure and pedicure £12 each; waxing from £4.50; electrolysis £5 per 1/2 hour.

Tariff

Special breaks are offered at Lucknam Park - these include accommodation for two nights, full English breakfast, à la carte dinner each evening, and full use of the Leisure Spa.

The rate per person sharing a twin/double room for the two nights is from £195; or £260 per person sharing a four poster room.

Travel Directions

From M4 exit at juntion 17 or 18 and follow signs to A420. Continue for 4 miles and at Ford turn onto Colerne road. Lucknam Park is 1/4 mile on the right.

Nearest railway station Bath 6 miles.

ENGLAND south west

POLURRIAN HOTEL CORNWALL

Polurrian Hotel
Mullion   Lizard Peninsula   Cornwall   TR12 7EN
☏ 0326 240421   Fx 0326 240083

| 40 | 🛏 ﹀ ✈ 📖 ≋ 🔍 🍽 £ |

Price category C

Dramatically situated 300 feet above its own secluded sandy cove in 12 acres of gardens and grounds, this friendly hotel is an ideal base for short healthy breaks or longer holidays. Polurrian has been owned and managed by the Francis family since 1947, and offers an excellent range of sporting and leisure facilities for all the family.

The new leisure club has a marble heated indoor pool, whirlpool spa, sauna, solarium and fully equipped gymnasium. There is a shop, children's playroom, teenage centre with video games, music centre and pool tables. Healthy snacks and refreshments are served in the Aqua Bar.

Charges in the leisure club: Gym, swimming pool and whirlpool spa, free; sauna £3 per 30 minutes; solarium £2.75 per 20 minutes or 10 sessions for £23; snooker 50p per 20 minutes; squash 50p per 25 minutes; aerobic classes £2 per hour.

Tennis, badminton, croquet and mini-golf are available on the premises, and for serious golfers an 18-hole golf course at Mullion is just 2 miles away. For swimmers there is a second heated pool outdoors and safe sea-bathing can be enjoyed from the hotel's own sandy cove and other beaches in this beautiful part of south Cornwall.

Bedrooms, some with stunning sea views, are well appointed with modern en suite bathrooms and baby-listening devices. Flowers and a glass of sherry on arrival are thoughtful welcoming touches. Some self-catering apartments and bungalows are available, all equipped down to the last teaspoon.

Menus using fresh fish caught by Polurrian's own boat can be enjoyed in the restaurant, as well as organically grown vegetables and salads from the hotel's greenhouses.

Cream teas served on the lawn are a popular feature on summer afternoons.

Treatments

A health and beauty studio offers hairdressing, health and beauty treatments - body massage £10 per 1/2 hour, £15 per hour, or £19 per 1 1/2 hours.

Reflexology treatments are also available at £19 for a 1 1/2 hour session.

Tariff

Nightly tariff per person sharing a double or twin-bedded en suite room, including full English breakfast and four course dinner, starts at £54 in room without sea view in early season, rising to £66 at Easter, £69 in early and late summer and £74 in high summer.

A standard sea view room costs from £62 in early season rising to £82 in high summer.

Weekly tariff for self-catering apartments and bungalows is based on four people sharing and starts at £139 per unit in spring and early autumn, £193 at Easter, £236 in summer/autumn, £275 at Whitsun and late summer, £376 in midsummer and £467 in high summer.

Travel Directions

From Helston follow A3083 signed to The Lizard for 6 miles, turn right onto B3296 to Mullion. Drive through village 1/2 mile to Mullion Cove.

Nearest railway station Redruth approximately 25 miles.

ENGLAND
central

ESTABLISHMENTS IN CENTRAL ENGLAND

Map ref.		Page no.
1	Belton Woods Hotel	114
2	Breadsall Priory	116
3	Elveden Forest - Center Parcs	118
4	Hinckley Island Hotel	121
5	Hoar Cross Hall	124
6	Lygon Arms	127
7	Malvern Nature Cure Centre	129
8	Mederi Centre	131
9	Norwich Sport Village	133
10	Ragdale Hall	135
11	Sherwood Forest - Center Parcs	138
12	Shrubland Hall	141
13	Springs Hydro	144
14	Sprowston Manor	146

ENGLAND central

BELTON WOODS HOTEL
LINCOLNSHIRE

Belton Woods Hotel
Belton   Nr Grantham   Lincolnshire   NG32 2LN
☎ 0476 593200   Fx 0476 74547

| 96 |

Price category C   A Scottish Highland Hotel

Belton Woods Hotel and Country Club is an exciting new development set amid 475 acres of parkland, lakes and golf courses. This fine new hotel offers luxury accommodation with use of the outstanding amenities of the private country club. These incorporate a large heated swimming pool with waterfalls and children's pool, spa bath with counter current exercise system, steam rooms, saunas, hairdressing and beauty salon, gym, snooker room, sports shop and two squash courts. Outdoor facilities include two 18-hole golf courses, 9-hole par 3 course, 24 bay floodlit driving range, putting green, two all-weather floodlit tennis courts, children's playground; clay pigeon shooting, trout fishing and nature trails for jogging or walking.

All bedrooms are furnished and equipped to a high standard, with private bathroom, satellite television, telephone, hair drier, trouser press and tea/coffee making facilities.

Guests have a choice of two restaurants for dining: the elegant Manor with specially created à la carte and table d'hôte menus, and Plus Fours for less formal dining and extensive choice of different dishes.

Treatments

An extensive selection of body and beauty treatments is available in the club's beauty salon.

Body treatments:

Full body massage £14; shoulder and back massage £10; leg massage £8; G5 massage £7; Dermatone faradic muscle toning £6.50; Kanebo body peel and moisture £20.

Beauty treatments:

Facials from £11; cleanse and make-up £8; make-up lesson £12; eyelash tinting £5; manicure with polish £5.50; pedicure £9; electrolysis £6; thread vein removal £6.95; millia removal £6.95; skin tag removal £6.95; waxing from £3; bleaching from £3.

A full range of hairdressing services is also available.

A *Top to Toe* day of beauty costs £55, and a pre holiday special £27.

Special beauty and pampering breaks are planned in the near future - for both sexes!

Tariff

Short weekend breaks are available throughout the year, and on any two nights during the months of July and August.

Rates are £55 per person per night, inclusive of accommodation, table d'hôte dinner and full English breakfast.

Regular accommodation tariff is £90 single or £110 double occupancy in a standard room, £110 single or £130 double occupancy in an Ambassador room (larger room overlooking the golf courses with extras such as bathrobe, complimentary newspaper, fresh flowers, chocolates, bidet and mini-bar).

The regular rates quoted are for bed and breakfast only.

Travel Directions

Travelling south - take A1 to Gonerby Moor Services, turn left to Great Gonerby then up hill, turning left to Manthorpe/Belton and left again onto A607.

Travelling north - follow A1 to Gonerby Moor Services (ignore signs to Grantham), and turn right onto B1174, and left at top of hill towards Manthorpe/Belton and left onto A607.

Nearest railway station Grantham approximately 3 miles.

ENGLAND central

BREADSALL PRIORY HOTEL
DERBYSHIRE

Breadsall Priory Hotel Golf and Country Club
Moor Road Morley Nr Derby Derbyshire DE7 6DL
☎ 0332 832235   Fx 0332 833509

92

Price category C   A Country Club Hotel

Breadsall Priory is a 13th century mansion set in 200 acres of mature parkland and approached by a long parkland drive. Its historic past is still much in evidence with battlements, huge doorways and tall elegant windows. Inside, log fires and a minstrel gallery complement modern amenities - bars, restaurant and leisure facilities. It is now one of ten Country Club Hotels offering similar leisure and sporting facilities.

All bedrooms are en suite with attractive furnishings and overlook the golf course or small courtyard.

Pre-dinner drinks can be enjoyed in front of the log fire in the Monk's Bar cocktail lounge, before trying the imaginative table d'hôte and à la carte menus in the Elizabethan Priory Restaurant.

The Golf and Country Club offers a whole range of excellent amenities. Indoors - a heated swimming pool, fitness studio, steam room, sauna, solarium, spa bath, three snooker tables, two squash courts and a poolside grill. Outdoors - children's play area, trim trail, two all-weather tennis courts, five-a-side football pitch and a challenging 18-hole - 6,011 yard golf course. A further 18-hole golf course is planned in the near future.

Indoor spa facilities are free of charge, apart from the sun beds which cost £3.50 per 20 minute session.

Sporting activities are charged at nominal rates, eg squash £2/£2.50 per session, tennis £3 per hour (floodlit £5), snooker £3, fitness studio £2. Golf fees are £18 Monday to Friday and £20 weekends and bank holidays, juniors £7.50.

Treatments

Body treatments:

Clarins body massage treatments - firming treatment, contouring treatment or exfoliating treatment take 45 minutes each and cost £17; body massage with infra-red £12.50 for 30 minutes;

Clarins bust treatment to improve position and firmness £10; faradic muscle toning to tone and firm slackened muscles £9 for 30 minutes or 6 for £50; G5 massage £9 for 1/2 hour or 6 for £50. The Clarins Paris Method is available as a facial £22, bust treatment £20, or body treatment £23 - each treatment designed to aid lymph drainage and circulation.

Beauty treatments:

Make-up £8.00; make-up with lesson £10; eye treatments from £3.50; Clarins 1 hour facial treatments £16 each; reviving 30 minute facial £9; manicure £8; pedicure £10.

The Health and Beauty Clinic also offers a complete *Health Farm Day*, available Monday to Friday at an inclusive cost of £55.

Tariff

Weekend breaks are available from approximately £60 per person per night for a minimum of two nights, and are inclusive of accommodation, breakfast and dinner.

Three night mid-week *Sneak-a-Breaks* cost approximately £200 per person for accommodation and meals.

(Exact rates not available when this book went to press.)

Travel Directions

3 miles north of Derby just off A38 on the edge of Breadsall village. Turn left at the off-licence and follow Moor Lane for 2 miles, Breadsall Priory is on the left.

ENGLAND
central

ELVEDEN FOREST
SUFFOLK

Center Parcs Elveden Forest Holiday Village
Brandon   Suffolk   IP27 0YZ
📞 0842 890000   0623 411 411 (reservations)

733 self catering villas   90 apartments

Elveden Forest opened in 1989 and is the second Center Parcs village in the UK. The villas and facilities are set in ancient Suffolk woodlands around attractively landscaped lakes. Thousands of trees and shrubs have been planted to conserve and encourage the wildlife population - Elveden Forest is home to the exotic golden pheasant and other rare species of birds and plants.

   Apart from the newly opened Country Club which is situated on the far side of the village, all the activities at Elveden Forest take place under one roof in the Parc Plaza. This futuristic leisure area incorporates tropical gardens with wildlife, rockpools and waterfalls, the Jardin des Sports - a huge indoor sports area, supermarket, shops, restaurants, bars, Spa and the Subtropical Swimming Paradise. This recreational pool is popular with all age groups and is open from 10 am until 9.45pm each day. Attractions include wildwater rapids, slow river, flumes, slides, salt pool and a wave pool. Small children have their own paddling pool, and there are whirlpools, solarium and poolside chairs for their parents' relaxation. Disabled visitors can also enjoy the Subtropical Swimming Paradise - changing cabins are provided and a service door by the shower area has easy access to the poolside.

Villas are modern and well equipped and have between one and four bedrooms. All are comfortable and warm having conventional and underfloor heating as well as provision for an open fire. Bed linen is provided, and towels can be hired on request. There are several villas with special provision for disabled visitors.

After unpacking, visitors are asked to leave their cars in the car parking areas to ensure the safety of bike riders and pedestrians in the village. Non-bikers should reserve villas within walking distance of the village centre, as some of the villas are quite a distance without transport.

For visitors who prefer apartment style living, the Sheldrake provides luxurious serviced accommodation - all double rooms have private bathroom with spa bath, television, radio and telephone. Breakfast is an optional extra which can be taken in the Sheldrake's restaurant, which is open to all Center Parc visitors.

At the top of the Sheldrake is Le Caprice, a revolving French restaurant with panoramic views of the village and an extensive choice of gourmet menus served by friendly staff.

Sports and Leisure Facilities

Apart from entry to the Parc Plaza and Subtropical Swimming Paradise, all 34 facilities are paid for as taken, ranging from £1.50 per session for table tennis to £15 per hour for windsurfing. Badminton, tennis and squash are especially popular sports and should be pre-booked a day in advance at the Activity Booking Desks. Most sports equipment can be hired for a nominal fee.

A bicycle is essential at Elveden Forest - everyone brings their own or hires one from the bike shop. Weekend charges are £7.50 for an adult bike, £4.10 for a child's bike, and £6.65 for a large BMX.

Spa Facilities

The Spa is situated next to the pool, and entry is via the pool or from the Jardin des Sports. This is a pleasant, restful area with two spacious saunas, steam room, plunge pools, drench pail, hot and cold showers, warm footbath, indoor and outdoor pool with hydro spa.

A token for entry to the Spa costs £6.15 for adults - children are admitted to family sessions only for £2 each.

An exhilarating cycle ride leads to Elveden Forest's brand new Country Club which opened in September 1991. The Club houses a French colonial style restaurant, snooker and tennis tables, dance studio and fitness room, children's play activity centre and a most attractive health and beauty salon - the Aqua Sana.

Treatments

The Aqua Sana offers a wide range of body and beauty treatments carried out in six pleasant treatment rooms which are open every day including Sunday.

Body treatments:

Seaweed body wrap £25; self-heating pack £10.25; therapeutic spa bath £19.50; aromatherapy £35.75; Vital Harmony £27; Algoceane £27; Affinoderm £27; bust care treatment £15; exfoliate massage £18; reflexology £25.55; Ionithermie £33.25; waxing from £3.60.

Beauty treatments:

Thalasso facial £11.15; Decleor Hollywood facial £40; Seborreor facial £32; holistic facials £28 each; Aromadermy facial £32; eyelash tint £5.70.

A full range of hairdressing services is available in the Aqua Sana's hair salon at various prices, eg wet hair cut and shampoo £6.50, perm £22 and £19.50 for highlights.

Tariff

Rates vary depending on time of year and villa size. A weekend stay (Friday afternoon until Monday morning) in early December in a two-bedroom villa costs £174 and rises to £351 for the August bank holiday weekend. The weekly rental for the same villa during the school summer holiday period when all villas are rented out weekly is £637.

A weekend in a Sheldrake apartment (two persons maximum) costs from £99 in early December to £228 for the August bank holiday weekend.

Travel Directions

Elveden Forest Holiday Village is reached via the motorway network to the A11 signposted Thetford and Norwich. Turn onto B1106 signposted Brandon and the entrance is half a mile on the left.

Detailed travel directions are sent with booking confirmation.

Nearest railway station Thetford approximately 4 miles.

HINCKLEY ISLAND HOTEL
LEICESTERSHIRE

ENGLAND central

Hinckley Island Hotel
Watling Street Hinckley Leicestershire LE10 3JA
☎ 0455 631122   Fx 0455 634536

|302|

Price category D

This comfortable, modern hotel in 13 acres of tranquil parkland and landscaped gardens complete with lake, is only yards from the motorway. Catering mainly for the business and conference market during the week, it offers good value for weekend breaks with guest facilities and services available seven days a week.

The outstanding attraction at Hinckley Island is the health and leisure complex, designed in Caribbean style with heated indoor kidney-shaped swimming pool, spa pool, Turkish bath, sauna, solarium, pool-side bar, beauty therapy rooms, hairdressing salon, dance studio, exercise and snooker rooms.

Hinckley Island has some unusual features for visitors to enjoy with lakeside activities such as boating and fishing. Hinckley is the home of the famous Hansom cab, and the Hinckley Hackney Carriage Museum is sited in the hotel grounds. The complex also includes a village shop and the Snooty Fox 'pub' designed on traditional lines with open fire and oak beams. A shopping plaza with 20 shops and children's créche is planned for the near future.

Bedrooms are well furnished with full en suite bathroom, satellite television, trouser press, hair drier, telephone, tea/coffee making facilities, radio and alarm call system. Child minding can be arranged.

Rooms equipped for the disabled visitor, de luxe rooms and suites are also available.

All tastes and appetites are catered for with a choice of four dining areas, plus 24 hour room service.

The Garden Coffee House is open all day and serves breakfast and other meals until 10pm; Hansom's restaurant is for more formal dining with à la carte menus; the Snooty Fox serves a range of hot dishes and salads, and light snacks and drinks are obtainable from the poolside bar.

Treatments

Decleor products are used for body and beauty treatments, and combine the principles of aromatherapy, acupressure and phytotherapy to combat skin and figure problems.

Body treatments:

Full body massage £16 and £10; neck and shoulder massage £7; waxing from £4; electrolysis from £3.50; body exfoliate massage £20; anti-cellulite treatment £17.50; leg care for poor circulation with aromatherapy oils, plant gel and relaxing massage £14.50; bust treatment £21; stretch mark treatment £17.50.

For a special occasion a complete body programme is recommended. This costs £40 and incorporates 1/2 hour body massage, Cleoderm facial, manicure, eyelash tint or eyebrow shape and day make-up.

Beauty treatments:

All facials begin with a diagnostic back massage - Decleor 5 Vitamin facials from £20 each or £95 for course of 5 treatments (one free); Triactive Aroma for mature or lined skins £30; make-up £10 and £12; eyelash tint £4.50; manicure £6.50; pedicure with leg and foot massage £8.50.

Masculine needs have not been overlooked at Hinckley Island with facials from £20; manicure £6.50; pedicure £8.50; 1/2 hour massage £10; neck and shoulder massage £7.

The unisex hairdressing salon offers an extensive range of System Professional treatments (from £4 for total conditioning treatment) and each client is given a personal diagnosis on their first visit. Prices for ordinary hairdressing such as cut and blow dry start at £9 for ladies and £6.50 for men.

Tariff

Two night weekend rates (must include a Saturday night) cost £45 per person sharing a double room. This rate includes dinner, bed and breakfast and full use of the leisure facilities (treatments extra). Single room supplement £5.

Travel Directions

Via motorway network to M69, exit at junction 1 and take A5 signed to Milton Keynes for 300 yards.

Nearest railway stations Hinckley (local) 1 mile, Nuneaton 5 miles, Leicester 12 miles.

ENGLAND central

HOAR CROSS HALL
STAFFORDSHIRE

Hoar Cross Hall
Hoar Cross   Nr Yoxall   Staffordshire   DE13 8QS
☏ 028375 671   Fx 028375 652

| 86 |

Price category B✽

Hoar Cross Hall - the health spa resort in a stately home as described in the brochure - opened in March 1991, and is an exciting new concept in British health spas.

The health and leisure resort is the brainchild of owner Steve Joynes, who has spent £8 million transforming his stately home into a luxurious spa based on continental lines.

Originally built in 1860 in 25 acres of woodlands and formal gardens between Abbots Bromley and Yoxall in rural Staffordshire, this Grade II listed building has been tastefully restored. Paintings and tapestries adorn the stylish rooms - an oak-panelled long gallery, banqueting hall and family chapel are unusual and interesting features.

The new and luxurious spa amenities are housed in a purpose built wing and include a cruciform shaped swimming pool, five hydrotherapy massage baths, relaxation area, floatarium, whirlpool spa, sauna, solaria, 30 treatment rooms, hairdressing salon, gym and exercise studio.

On arrival all guests are given a tour of Hoar Cross Hall, a treatment consultation and blood pressure check.

Many of the bedrooms have lovely views over the gardens and are complete with en suite bathroom, television, beverage tray, fruit basket, fresh flowers and daily newspaper. The daily rate includes breakfast, lunch and dinner and complimentary beverages throughout the day.

Food at Hoar Cross Hall is exceptionally good - delicious healthy breakfasts and delectable lunches served beside the pool, followed by dinner in a traditional candle-lit dining room, complete with ornate gilded ceilings, crystal chandeliers and Louis style furniture. Menu choice is excellent and includes fresh fish and vegetarian choices as well as prime cuts of beef, lamb and chicken carefully prepared and served with salad or lightly cooked vegetables. Most types of diet can be catered for and weight watchers can select courses from a green calorie coded menu.

Pre-dinner drinks can be taken in the original library, discreetly transformed into a champagne and cocktail bar.

Residents have unlimited use of the hydrotherapy pool and whirlpool spa, steam room, sauna and sporting amenities such as 9-hole golf improvement course, outdoor tennis and badminton, croquet green, gym, exercise studio, boules and bicycles. Free activities such as aerobics, tummy trimming, hydrotherapy pool exercises, gentle gym, circuit training, relaxation and walks are held daily.

Evening talks, videos and demonstrations on health, beauty and fitness topics are also included in the tariff

Treatments

Hoar Cross Hall specialises in thalassotherapy (treatments using sea products) to invigorate and rejuvenate. A complete marine programme costs £60 and consists of marine algae hydrotherapy bath, full body seaweed envelopment and a blitz jet douche.

Body treatments:

Body massage £18 per 1/2 hour; aromatherapy £36; facials for men and women from £20; faradic body toning £10.50; mud hydrotherapy massage bath £30; full body mud envelopment £28; G5 massage; Cellu M6 treatments from £26; waxing from £6.50; reflexology £25; individual steam cabinet £6; high intensity sunbed £13.50, etc.

Beauty treatments:
Facials from £20; manicure £12; pedicure £13; make-up £13; eyelash or eyebrow tint £8.50, etc.

The hair studio offers a full range of hairdressing services with prices ranging from £4.50 for a dry cut to £45 for highlights.

Tariff

Two nights is the minimum length for a residential stay.

Rates are per person sharing double accommodation - £95 per night for a superior room, £115 for a luxury master bedroom and £125 for a suite. Single supplement £20 daily.

This rate includes all meals and beverages throughout the day, body salt rub, thalassotherapy massage bath, body massage, G5 or back massage with infra red and use of all amenities.

The longer the stay the greater the number of inclusive treatments, eg - the five night stay includes 2 body salt rubs, 2 thalassotherapy massage baths, 3 body massages, G5 or back massages with infra red, 1 hair and scalp treatment and 1 solarium.

One day packages are offered to non-resident guests. All include a welcoming tour and blood pressure check, unlimited use of leisure facilities, lunch in the poolside restaurant and complimentary beverages throughout the day.

Special Relaxation Day £33; *Beauty Treat Day* including treatments £68; *Body Treat Day* with body treatments £68; and *Top to Toe Day* incorporating beauty, hair and body treatments £88.

Travel Directions

Follow motorway network to A515.

From north follow signs to Lichfield, turning right after Draycott in the Clay and onto unclassified road to Hoar Cross.

From south follow A515 signed to Ashbourne and turn left after Yoxall turning left onto unclassified road to Hoar Cross.

Nearest railway station Lichfield 10 miles.

THE LYGON ARMS
HEREFORD & WORCESTER

ENGLAND central

The Lygon Arms
Broadway   Hereford & Worcester   WR12 7DU
☎ 0386 852255   Fx 0386 858611

63

Price category B   A Savoy Group Hotel

This former Elizabethan country inn stands in the middle of the pretty Cotswold village of Broadway. It has been offering hospitality for over 450 years, and is now a comfortable and welcoming hotel, combining today's luxuries alongside historic reminders of its long history. There are wonderful inglenook fireplaces, cosy public rooms and some period bedrooms complete with four poster beds.

A newly opened leisure club is the last word in relaxation and comfort, and offers guests a wide range of superb facilities. There is a luxurious swimming pool with adjacent spa bath, separate saunas with plunge pools, steam room, two modern solaria with CD systems, hair and beauty salons, treatment rooms, fitness studio and billiards room. A spiral staircase from the pool leads to the upper lounge and adjoining roof garden, where drinks and light meals can be taken overlooking the pool.

Outside there is an all-weather floodlit tennis court, with rackets and balls provided. Informative jogging/walking maps of the area can be obtained from reception.

Luxurious accommodation is in either the period bedrooms of the original inn or the modern guest rooms of the Garden and Orchard wings. All rooms have en suite bathroom, bathrobes, hair drier, telephone and television.

The Great Hall Restaurant complete with minstrel's gallery, offers traditional high quality cuisine. In summer informal meals can be taken in the garden courtyard Patio Restaurant.

Treatments

Treatments are carried out in the pleasant surroundings of the new Country Club which has treatment rooms and a hair and beauty salon.

Body treatments:

Cathiodermie bust treatments £25; Elemis aromatic massage £28; Elemis back/shoulder massage £18; faradic toning £17 per session or 6 for £85; G5 massage £16 or 6 for £80.

Beauty treatments:

A full range of beauty treatments is available including René Guinot Cathiodermie facial £28; Elemis de-sensitising facial £26; aromatherapy eye treatment £15 or 3 for £40; manicure £12, pedicure £14, eyelash tinting £9; make-up £14; waxing from £6 and electrolysis from £10.

Special health and beauty specials are £40, fitness assessment and lifestyle evaluations cost from £20, individual exercise programmes from £10.

Tariff

A mid-week Cotswold break at the Lygon Arms for two nights Sunday to Thursday inclusive is £185 per person. This includes luxury double or twin bedded room, early morning tea and copy of the Daily Telegraph, full English breakfast each morning, table d'hôte dinner each evening, and full use of the leisure facilities (treatments extra).

Travel Directions

Take M40 to Oxford then A40 to Burford. At Burford turn onto A424 towards Stow-on-the-Wold for 15 miles, picking up A44 to Broadway.

Nearest railway stations Evesham 5 miles, Moreton-in-Marsh 8 miles.

MALVERN CENTRE
HEREFORD & WORCESTER

**ENGLAND
central**

Malvern Nature Cure Centre
5 College Grove   Great Malvern   Hereford & Worcester   WR14 3HP
☎ 0684 566818

| 8 |  |

Price category D✻

This pleasant house, recently renovated, stands in half an acre of garden in the Regency town of Malvern. Situated in a quiet cul de sac with panoramic views front and back, the Centre is a ten minute walk from the spa town and its many attractions for the visitor - Winter Gardens, Lido, Festival Theatre, shops and parks - a good choice for a quiet holiday in an area where the surrounding hills lend themselves to walking and touring.

   The Centre provides a skilled and reasonably priced Nature Cure treatment, for those wanting help and guidance in their search for good health or recovery from illness.

All bedrooms are centrally heated with comfortable Slumberland Orthofirm bed, electric blanket, wash-basin and television. There are no en suite rooms, bathroom facilities are shared.

The Centre's cuisine is lacto-ovo-vegetarian, with all dairy produce except daily delivery of milk obtained from organic suppliers. All water used in fasting is Malvern spring water. Except in the short term (three or four days), individual vegan, gluten-free and other 'allergy-free' diets, or the Hay diet, cannot be supplied.

Slimmers are catered for here with an appetising but restricted dietary regime and nutritional guidance.

Visitors are encouraged to use Malvern's new indoor swimming pool, just three minutes away by car. The therapeutic brine baths at Droitwich are just 15 miles away, and provide a marvellous opportunity to enjoy relaxation and weightless exercise in a unique environment similar to the Dead Sea.

Treatments

To take full advantage of the treatments offered, it is advised to book in as a 'patient' rather than a 'guest'. The special weekly treatments package costs £85 per week, plus an additional consultation fee and includes daily manipulation/massage, 1 hour relaxation session, 3 discussions or Question and Answer group sessions given by a practitioner and lasting an hour, 1 sunbed or vibro bed, 1 vegetarian cookery demonstration and 1 remedial exercise class.

Tariff

Accommodation rates depend on season and room situation. Visitors booking in as 'patients' are expected to take the full board tariff, 'guests' can opt for bed/breakfast, half or full board, but do not have the benefit of treatments.

A room on the first floor during the high season (March to end of October and 23 December to 1 January) costs £30.25 per day full board, £25.75 half board and £18.25 bed and breakfast per person.

Other facilities at the Centre include sunbed £2.50 per session; specific remedial exercises by trained gymnast £4.50 per 1/2 hour; individual relaxation tuition £7.50 per hour (ladies only), and vibro bed £2.50 per 1/2 hour session.

Malvern Nature Cure Centre's brochure promises "a pleasant environment where both the healthy and sick seek sanctuary and help and where they can enjoy the varied amenities that Malvern offers."

Travel Directions

From M5 exit at junction 7 taking A449 to Great Malvern, or if travelling from the east, A4103, B4219 and A449. Follow signs to Malvern College.

Nearest railway station Great Malvern Station less than a mile.

MEDERI CENTRE
SHROPSHIRE

ENGLAND central

Mederi Centre
Southfield Road   Much Wenlock   Shropshire   TF13 6AT
☏ 0952 727245   Fx 0952 727191

| 30 | ☆ | ◊ | ≋ | ☯ | ☺ | 🍇 | ≋ | 大 |

Price category C✷

The Mederi Centre is situated in the pleasant small town of Much Wenlock in the heart of rural Shropshire, and aims to promote a balanced lifestyle through natural therapies and health guidance.

Newly opened in February 1991, it offers a peaceful retreat with homely accommodation, vegetarian cuisine, spa facilities and alternative health treatment and workshops.

Facilities include a warm indoor pool with steps at the shallow end and a hydraulic chair if required, jacuzzi, sauna, solarium steam room and floatation tank.

Disabled visitors will be pleased to note that every facility at Mederi has been designed to meet their needs and allow special ease of access.

Comfortable bedrooms are furnished in natural wood and fabrics, and have either twin or triple beds, en suite bathroom, telephone, satellite television, alarm call system and hi fi.

Although the cuisine is vegetarian, the chef can cater for all needs and special diets. Non-vegetarian meals cost an additional £2.50 per meal.

Treatments

No beauty treatments here, just an extensive range of holistic therapies including acupuncture, therapeutic massage, homoeopathy, aromatherapy, reflexology, shiatsu, yoga, meditation and many more.

Medical herbalist Kitty Campion and other well known therapists run residential courses throughout the year, and special therapy weekends are available from Friday lunchtime until after lunch on Sunday.

Tariff

The *Special Therapy Weekend* costs £125 per person, and is inclusive of dinner, bed and continental breakfast, swimming and use of facilities at specified times, choice of two individual therapies available on the weekend, and callanetics/exercise/yoga classes.

Additional therapies are available at a cost of £15 per session. Extra nights can also be reserved for £45 per person inclusive of accommodation and breakfast.

Travel Directions

Take M54 to junction 6 and A4169 to Much Wenlock. The Centre is a short distance from the town centre on Southfield Road.

Nearest railway station Telford approximately 10 miles.

NORWICH SPORT VILLAGE
NORFOLK

ENGLAND central

Norwich Sport Village and Hotel
Drayton High Road   Norwich   Norfolk   NR6 5DU
© 0603 788898   Fx 0603 406845

| 55 |

Price category D

This is the ultimate in sport and leisure facilities for all the family, a totally self contained leisure village comprising a modern hotel with two restaurants and bars, sports shop, and possibly the best sporting complex in the UK - including a brand new £4.5 million aquapark.

The modern health and fitness centre has relaxation pool, spa bath, steam bath, sauna, alpine solarium, multigym, aerobics, massage, beauty clinics and free exercise area.

The extensive sporting facilities can be booked up to 14 days in advance and include 7 indoor tennis courts, 5 outdoor all weather tennis courts, 7 squash courts, 16 badminton courts and 9 full sized snooker tables.

The multi-sports hall is used for volleyball, five-a-side football, short tennis, hockey, netball, table tennis and short mat bowls. Prices are reasonable and equipment can be hired from the village Pro Shop at competitive rates.

Fitness assessments in the gym cost £8.50 per person, and individual work-outs are priced according to time of day, from £1.75 to £3.

There is a varied timetable of exercise classes throughout the week at £2 to £3 per session.

The Sport Village Hotel has reasonable rates for comfortable modern en suite accommodation, and prices include full English breakfast and access to the sporting facilities. Guests have free entrance to the swimming pool and new aquapark, with all sporting activities and facilities on a reasonable pay-as-you-use basis.

Treatments

Body massage 1 hour £15; 6 x G5 massages £45; 6 Slendertone treatments £45; *Mini-Top-to-Toe* £27.50 including back massage, mini deep cleansing facial, manicure and pedicure 3 hours; *Top-to-Toe* package £45 including full body massage, full facial, eyelash tint, eyebrow shape, luxury manicure and pedicure.

A range of facials are available using Clarins products with prices from £7 for 1/2 hour treatment. Waxing from £5, and electrolysis from £4.50 are also available. Manicure and pedicure charges from £6.50.

Tariff

Sport, health and leisure weekends are available from £89 per person sharing a twin room, and include breakfast, evening meal and sports pass.

Regular mid-week tariff starts at £59 per night single or £69 double room (two persons) with breakfast. Half board tariff mid-week is £65 single and £89 double room (two persons).

No charge for children under 14 sharing room with parents, and 50% reduction in meals.

Travel Directions

The complex is situated on A1067 Drayton High Road, north west of the city of Norwich.

Nearest railway station Norwich approximately 2 miles.

RAGDALE HALL
LEICESTERSHIRE

ENGLAND central

Ragdale Hall Health Hydro
Ragdale   Nr Melton Mowbray   Leicestershire   LE14 3PB
☏ 0664 434831/434411   Fx 0664 434587

Price category B✲

This popular health hydro is set in a country manor house amid the rolling Leicestershire countryside. Originally established in the 1970s it has recently had a change of ownership and a £3.5 million refit and renovation, which has improved accommodation and facilities enormously.

 The new spa area keeps dry and wet treatment areas separate, and has sauna, steam room, jacuzzi, plunge pool, floatation tank and underwater massage facilities with copious supplies of soft white towels. The improvements have also re-located the gym, exercise studio, sun centre and hair studio. The newly created Garden Room and Conservatory is filled with exotic plants in enormous pottery tubs and comfortable cane furniture. It is a delightful area in which to relax and enjoy a soft drink after exercise.

On arrival, there is a consultation with a senior therapist to plan a personal programme of treatments followed by a visit to the dietician. A health check questionnaire is completed to ensure all treatments prescribed are individually safe.

All bedrooms have en suite facilities, telephone, television and hair drier and are furnished and decorated to a high standard. Breakfast is served on a tray in your room each morning between 7.30am and 8.00am (no chance of a lie-in!).

Lunch and dinner are taken in the cosy and pleasantly sociable dining room with lots of vegetarian food choices included on the menu. At dinner, there is a choice of two main courses and all food is helpfully calorie counted, with an appetising 1100 calorie diet available for slimmers. Food is well prepared and plentiful - freshly baked rolls *and* jacket potatoes at lunch (plus a substantial main course and unlimited helping of salad) and a four course dinner in the evening. Guests can drink wine with their meals if they wish. Coffee and tea (extra charge) are taken in the Garden Room.

No smoking is allowed in the public rooms or bedrooms - smokers are asked to retreat to the smokers' lounge if the urge to smoke becomes unbearable.

Ragdale Hall does not accept guests wishing to fast, anorexia nervosa sufferers or anyone aged under 16 years.

All treatments and facilities are available seven days a week, so Sunday treatments are definitely 'on'!

Tracksuits and informal leisurewear are worn by everyone - there is no need to dress up at any time. One or more swimsuits are essential to make the most of the super water facilities, including both the indoor and outdoor (summer only) pools. Boutiques in the hydro sell fashionable swimwear, tracksuits and accessories, as well as natural remedies and beauty products.

Treatments

There are over 80 optional treatments that can be booked at the time of making reservations.

Body treatments:

Aromatherapy £38.50; Cleotherm body wrap £21.50; Ionithermie £38.50 or £68 for two sessions; Cellu M6 stress relief treatment £20.50; G5 massage £12.50; reflexology £34; ultrasun sunbed from £15.

Beauty treatments:

Ragdale facial £12.50; Cathiodermie facial £35; men's facial £12; manicure £14.50; pedicure £16.50; Kanebo Esthe facial with shiatsu £34; make-up and lesson £22.75; eyelash tint £10.50.

Other facilities:
Computerised fitness evaluation £26; metabolic rate test from £26; cholesterol test and advice £14.50.

A full selection of hairdressing services and treatments is available in the Hair Salon - hair consultations are free.

Tariff

All stays include accommodation, breakfast tray, buffet lunch and dinner; consultation with Health, Sports and Beauty Departments.

The number of treatments included in the tariff depends on the length of stay from 14 treatments on a seven night stay to 3 on a two night stay.

Accommodation is divided into five types due to size of room, comfort and location. Prices start at £112.50 per night for a *Standard* single room with shower and wc or £89.50 per person sharing; *Standard Plus* room with bath, shower and wc is £121.50 single or £99.50 per person sharing; *Superior* room with bath, shower and wc is £137.50 single or £109.50 per person sharing; *Superior Plus* room with bath, shower, bidet and wc is £154.50 single or £125 per person sharing; *Suites* £184.50 for single occupancy per night or £146 per person sharing

The tariff also includes use of the spa area with sauna, steam room, whirlpool bath, swimming pool, scheduled exercise classes, gym, recreational facilities and evening talks.

A range of non-residential day packages are available and offer full use of all sports and recreational facilities as well as lunch and specified treatments.

The *Standard* day guest package costs £52 and includes three treatments; the *Beauty* package £83 includes four treatments; the *Body and Fitness* £83 includes G5 massage, personal exercise programme in gym, fitness assessment and individual sports coaching.

Ragdale Hall is a very friendly establishment with a caring staff and the emphasis firmly on relaxation and feeling good.

Travel Directions

From M1 exit at junction 23 taking A512 to Loughborough. From Loughborough take B676 to Melton Mowbray for 7 miles, passing under bridge carrying A46. Ragdale Hall is about 1/2 mile from the bridge on the right.

From A1, turn off at Stamford (A606) or Grantham (A607) and head for Melton Mowbray. Follow signs to Loughborough and B676 for 7 miles then follow signs on left for Ragdale Hall.

Nearest railway station: Leicester 12 miles.

ENGLAND central

SHERWOOD FOREST
NOTTINGHAMSHIRE

**Center Parcs Sherwood Forest Holiday Village
Rufford   Nottinghamshire   NG22 9DN**
☏ 0272 244 744 (brochure) 0623 411 411 (reservations)

709 self catering villas

Sherwood Forest - the UK's first Center Parc holiday village - is situated amid 400 acres of woodlands and lakes in the heart of rural Nottinghamshire. Open 365 days a year, it offers an exceptional range of sports and leisure activities that can be enjoyed whatever the weather.

  Accommodation is in groups of bright modern villas situated in woodlands and around the lakes, well designed to maximise privacy without being isolated.

  After unpacking, visitors are requested to drive their cars to special parking areas, to ensure a traffic-free village with roads safe for pedestrians and bicycles. Just about everyone - young and old - hires a bicycle for the duration of their stay, and the wide safe roads make cycling a pleasure. Non-bikers should reserve villas near the centre of the village so all the different activities and shops are within easy walking distance.

The holiday village accommodates about 3,000 guests in comfortable self-catering villas which vary in size from one to four bedrooms. The villas are roomy and well equipped with modern appliances, central heating and double glazing.

The rental includes use of the villa and all its services, including video films, electricity, gas, heating and bedlinen, and free entry to the Subtropical Swimming Paradise.

Rentals do not include meals, and separate charges are made for all other facilities and services. Trying lots of activities can be expensive so bringing your own sports equipment helps keep costs down.

Examples of Equipment Hire & Sports Charges

Bicycle hire adult £3.60 daily, £7.15 weekend, £11.25 week; BMX (large) £3.35 daily, £6.65 weekend, £10.75 week; badminton £3.60; squash £2.35; tennis outdoor £3.40; indoor £10.25; (racket hire £1); soccer school session £4.60; pony trekking £8.70; aerobics £2.10; snooker £3.10 per hour, etc, etc.

The range of shops in the village includes a supermarket, restaurants, grills, bars, coffee shops, ice cream parlours and a launderette - all are open seven days a week and until late in the evenings on visitor-arrival days.

Sports & Leisure Facilities

Sherwood Forest has an outstanding range of outdoor pursuits - archery, pony riding, soccer and soccer coaching, tennis, canoeing, jogging, putting, golf driving range and volleyball - the choice is staggering.

Facilities indoors are equally impressive with aerobics, fitness and weight training, rollerskating, tennis, snooker, squash, fencing and table tennis to name but a few!

Main focus at Sherwood Forest is the Subtropical Swimming Paradise, with its tropical landscape of palms and lush vegetation, tumbling cascades of water, wild water rapids, drifting lazy river, and bubbling whirlpool spa - all in a constant year round temperature of 84°F.

A warning is sounded before the calm pool waters are transformed into a surging swell by the wave machine - less confident bathers should be in the shallow end for safety as the waters get very turbulent. Other water rides such as the lazy river drift and wild water rapids are also great fun, as are the two whirlpools baths beside the main pool.

Little children enjoy a separate shallow water pool with wheeled playpens and buoyancy aids.

Spa Facilities

The Spa area adjoins the pool and is accessible only via the main pool, which is inconvenient. Spa and sunbed bookings are made at the reception desk in the pool area, which again is accessible only to those in swimsuits and bare feet. Despite the inconvenience gaining entry, the Spa has excellent facilities and includes in and outdoor saunas and swimming pools, plunge pool, steam bath, sun beds (£5 extra), foot spa and relaxation area.

Family, ladies' only and mixed sessions are held in the Spa, where the entrance fee of £6.15 includes complimentary soft drinks and towel hire. Under 14s can use the Spa during the family sessions - entrance charge for under 14s is £1.50.

Treatments

The Aqua Sana health and leisure facility offers a range of body and beauty treatments including some continental ones unique to Centre Parcs such as Karwendel - a therapeutic bath using fossil oils and especially effective for skin disorders. A session of this enjoyable treatment costs £17.95. The Aqua Sana features thalassotherapy treatments and the latest relaxation therapy - floatation - where a session in one of the shallow warm pools costs £11.25. Other treatments include seaweed body wrap £22.50; aromatherapy £35 for 1½ hour treatment; reflexology £25.55; thalasso facial from £9.90; Ionithermie body treatment £33.25; quick-tanner sunbed £6.15; manicure £9; pedicure £12.50; eyelash treatments from £4.95.
A full range of hair care treatments as well as colouring, perming and styling is available in the hair salon in the Aqua Sana.

Several one-day beauty packages are available Mondays and Fridays from £21 to £76.70.

Tariff

Villas can be booked for whole weeks (start and finish on Fridays), mid-week breaks (start on Monday finish on Friday), or weekends (start on Friday finish on Monday), and rental costs vary with the size of villa and the time of year.

A weekend break in a 2 bedroom villa (four persons) in early January costs £167 and rises to £275 at the end of May. During July and August when rentals are on a weekly only basis the rate would be £595.

Reservations are made ONLY by telephone on the above number - no postal bookings.

Travel Directions

Sherwood Forest Holiday Village is located at Rufford, near Newark in Nottinghamshire, approximately 25 minutes drive from M1 and A1 on the B6034. Full travel directions sent with booking confirmation.

Nearest railway station (mainline) Newark approximately 12 miles.

SHRUBLAND HALL
SUFFOLK

ENGLAND central

Shrubland Hall Health Clinic
Coddenham   Nr Ipswich   Suffolk   IP6 9QH
℡   0473 830404

Price category B✻

Shrubland Hall's impressive Georgian manor house dates back to 1740 and enjoys extensive views across the Suffolk countryside. Visiting this health clinic is like being welcomed into a gracious stately home, with every effort made to ensure guests are as comfortable and well informed about their diets and treatments as possible.

The lovely ten acre grounds are a delightful mix of wild gardens, woodlands - some trees are over 800 years old - and spectacular terraced formal gardens laid out in classical style.

Shrubland Hall was converted into a health clinic in 1966, and chosen for the opening sequences of the James Bond movie, *Never Say Never Again*. This boosted male attendance at health farms overnight and led to health farms establishing health and fitness programmes geared to men's special needs, especially those of the busy executive with a stressed lifestyle.

Shrubland Hall's aim is to assist guests (referred to as patients) in restoring full health potential by providing a tranquil and supportive atmosphere where treatments and therapies are given according to need. The emphasis is firmly on unwinding, rest and relaxation.

All food is vegetarian and no cooked meals are available.

A light breakfast is served in your room each morning. Lunch and dinner consist of exotic and colourful salads, raw fruit, vegetable soups and broths, together with home made yoghurt, cheese and wholewheat bread baked from the estate's own barley and wheat. No alcohol is served in the dining room but visitors can enjoy drinking the fresh water from Shrubland Hall's own well. Complete fasts on liquid or light diet are supervised and well supported by a caring and attentive staff.

A total of 51 visitors can be accommodated - 38 in the main house and the remainder in an interesting assortment of locations. The main house has a lift to all floors and room prices vary according to size, location and amenities - there are two four poster rooms and 21 rooms with en suite facilities.

Old Hall, half a mile from the main house is in the heart of the Park and has six attractive bedrooms. Bicycles are available for hire, although use of a car is recommended as other than breakfast (served in the bedrooms by the resident housekeeper), all other activities and meals are in the main house. Just 50 yards from the main house are the Garden Rooms - all with en suite facilities and excellent views.

Russian Lodge is an attractive timber cottage in its own garden some 200 yards from the main house - it has two single rooms and a sitting room, cheerfully furnished and well heated, as well as a small kitchen and a bathroom.

Sports facilities include tennis, gym, billiard room, swimming pools (indoor and out) and fishing.

Wholesome food items to take home are available from the produce shop, there are other shops selling herbal preparations and beauty products, as well as a large range of tracksuits, robes and swimwear.

Treatments

Shortly after arrival, every visitor is given a thorough medical examination by one of clinic's doctors, and an individual programme of diet and treatments prescribed or recommended. Such treatments might include massage, Kneipp therapy, sauna, steam cabinet, underwater massage, aquarobic, yoga or exercise classes.

A floatation tank has recently been added to the amenities, and costs £17 a session - at least two sessions are recommended for maximum benefit. Other specialised treatments that can be recommended by the doctor include manipulative therapies, postural re-education, private relaxation instruction, physiotherapy and colonic irrigation.

Optional body and beauty treatments include reflexology £19.50; aromatherapy £27.50; seaweed body wrap £27.50; Alexander Technique £25; Clarins Paris facial £27.50; Clarins bust treatment £16.50; body wax £27.50.

Hairdressing is also available.

No body and beauty treatments given on Sundays.

Tariff

The tariff includes accommodation, consultations (all new patients see doctor, sister and dietician), daily heat treatment (sauna, steam cabinet or Turkish bath), body massage (manual or underwater) plus daily exercise class and use of sporting and leisure facilities.

A week's stay (six nights) in a single room costs from £380 to £590, and the price per person sharing a double room for the same period is from £425 to £435 per person. Arrival is on a Sunday or Wednesday afternoon.

Shorter breaks have recently been introduced at Shrubland Hall and cost from £275 for a three night stay or from £330 for four nights.

Please note these prices DO NOT include VAT which is added to all accounts at the current rate.

Travel Directions

Via motorway network towards Ipswich on A45. Shrubland Hall is north of Ipswich, exit at B113 signed to Great Blakenham and drive on through Claydon. Shrubland Hall is after the village.

Nearest railway station Ipswich 6 miles.

ENGLAND central

SPRINGS HYDRO
LEICESTERSHIRE

Springs Hydro
Arlick Farm Packington Nr Ashby de la Zouch Leicestershire LE6 5TG
ⓒ 0530 273873   (Fx) 0530 270987

| 41 |

Price category C✽

Springs opened in August 1990 and is Britain's first purpose built health hydro, offering a wide range of water facilities, including saunas, steam room, whirlpool spa, swimming pool, splash and plunge pools and a floatation room.

Recently acquired by the Purdew family, owners of Henlow Grange, Springs enjoys a countryside setting in rural Leicestershire. Modern luxury and convenience are combined with an extensive range of exercise classes, evening talks and optional body and beauty treatments. Accommodation is in spacious, modern rooms with en suite facilities with either a patio or balcony. Superior rooms have whirlpool bath, bidet and separate pulsar shower.

Food is wholesome and organic whenever possible, with a selection of organic wines served with the table d'hôte lunch and dinner menus.

There are cosy open fires in the lounges, ideal for relaxing by after dinner with a good book, or the more actively inclined can enjoy using the free floodlit tennis court. Mountain bikes can be hired (details at Reception); a basket of balls on the golf range is £3.50. Archery, squash and horses-riding can be arranged locally.

Treatments

Body treatments:

Aromatherapy £32; aroma and reflex zone £50.50; G5 massage £10.50; Slendertone £12.50; Swedish massage £14.50; Decleor Vital Harmony £27.50; Thalgo hydrotherapy £30.50; floatation £20; waxing from £11.75; sunbed £5, UVA sunbed £16.50; toning table £10.25.

Beauty treatments:

Cathiodermie £33; Hollywood facial £35; Prescription facial £19.50; manicure £14.50; pedicure £13.50; make-up consultation £10.50.

Tariff

The tariff includes a consultation on arrival and one full body massage daily, as well as unlimited use of all sports and water facilities, exercise classes, talks and demonstrations.

Standard room is £89.50 per night single, or £67.50 per person sharing double or twin room. *Studio* room is £99.50 per night single, £79.50 per person sharing double or twin room. *Superior Studio* room with whirlpool bath, bidet, separate pulsar shower and fresh fruit basket £109.50 per night single or £89.50 per person sharing double or twin room.

Inclusive short break packages are offered throughout the year:

Five Night Special includes all meals, consultation on arrival, three full body massages, one facial or neck shoulder massage, one G5 massage and unlimited use of all facilities including sauna and steam room and exercise and relaxation programme.

£265 per person sharing twin/double standard room or £315 per person sharing studio room.

Non-residential days are available from £24.95.

Travel Directions

From M1 exit at junction 22 and follow signs for A50 Burton-on-Trent. Take A42/M42 South and follow signs for Snarestone B4116.

From west, follow M42/A42 North then take B5006 Ashby exit, and follow signs for Snarestone B4116.

Nearest railway station Burton-on-Trent 12 miles, Loughborough 14 miles.

ENGLAND central

SPROWSTON MANOR HOTEL
NORFOLK

Sprowston Manor Hotel
Wroxham Road   Norwich   Norfolk   NR7 8RP
☎ 0603 410871   Fx 0603 423911

|117|

Price category D

An avenue lined with oak trees leads to historic Sprowston Manor, a historic 19th century country house with origins dating back over 400 years. Situated in ten acres of parkland adjoining a golf course, it has recently undergone a major transformation, with the building of a new wing with 87 executive bedrooms and a state of the art leisure club. The new wing complements the 36 bedrooms in the main house, which have all been refurbished to a high standard.

All the luxurious bedrooms are double rooms and have en suite bathroom, bathrobes, satellite television, telephone, tea/coffee making facilities, trouser press and hair drier.

Traditional English and French cuisine is served at lunch and dinner in the Manor Restaurant and Orangery. In winter, pre-dinner drinks can be enjoyed by an open fire in the adjoining Gurney Bar, or on the garden terrace in fine weather.

The new Sprowston Manor Leisure Club is open to hotel residents and a selected club membership. Designed in tropical style, the club has a large heated swimming pool, king size spa bath and children's lagoon with two steam rooms, sauna, solarium, gym, beauty salon and pool-side bar selling soft drinks and health food snacks.

Sprowston Manor adjoins an 18-hole golf course, and residents can have a round of golf during the week for £10 or on the weekends for £12.

All areas of the hotel and the swimming pool area of the Leisure Club are accessible to wheelchairs, by lift or ramp.

Treatments

An exclusive range of Sisley French botanical beauty products is used in La Fontana beauty salon, which offers facial and body treatments.

Body treatments:

Sauna and steam bath £2.50 each; body massage £20 per hour; G5 massage £9 for 30 minutes or 6 for £50; intensive bust care treatment £12; aromatherapy £30; paraffin wax treatments from £18; solarium £5.

Beauty treatments:

Sisley Aromatique Essential facial starts with a relaxing back massage followed by a thorough facial using essential oils, and massage to the hands, arms, feet and legs. The treatment ends with a personally designed make-up and costs £30.

Other beauty treats include facials from £15; manicure and hand massage £6.50; pedicure with foot and leg massage £10; eyelash tint £6; waxing from £3.50; electrolysis from £6.75.

Two health and beauty packages are offered costing £95 each.

The *Health and Slimming Day* includes consultation with therapist, heat treatment and refreshments, sunbed and shower, healthy lunch, faradic slimming treatment, make-up or manicure.

The *Health and Beauty Day* includes Essential Aromatique treatment, de luxe manicure, de luxe pedicure, sun bed, healthy lunch, make-up.

Tariff

Weekend *Getaway* breaks are good value at Sprowston Manor, and are for a minimum of two nights starting on a Friday or Saturday and include accommodation, full English breakfast, table d'hôte dinner and membership of the Leisure Club during stay. The break costs

£49.50 per person per night, four poster rooms and suites available for £10 extra per person per night.

Regular mid-week and single night tariff including English breakfast is from £81 for single occupancy or £91 double occupancy.

Travel Directions
From the Norwich northern ring road take A1151 Wroxham Road, the hotel is 1 1/2 miles on the right.

Nearest railway station Norwich 4 miles

SPAS and HEALTH FARMS for PREVENTION AND FITNESS

A visit to a European Spa or a health farm in Britain or in the USA will help you to stay fit or to recover from stress, after an accident or an operation. We can assist you with reservations and travel.

For Thalasso Therapy: Thalezur Spa Centre at Antibes nr Nice, Hotel Miramar at Biarritz; 5 Thalasso centres in Brittany.

For hydrotherapy, relaxation, slimming, diet, recovery from stress: The leading spas of Switzerland (Baden bei Zurich, Leukerbad, Bad Ragaz, St. Moritz) and Yverdon-les-Bains; Klassis Hotel, nr Istanbul, Turkey.

Treatment for rheumatism and arthritis (Fango-Mudpack): Abano/Montegrotto (nr. Padua) Italy, Jolly Hotels in Ischia and Taormina.

For excellent value and first rate medical supervision and hot thermal springs: Czech, Slovak and Hungarian spas. Special rehabilitation clinic at Dudince.

Beauty treatment, fitness, sport, relaxation. Health Farms in Britain and the USA.

ERNA LOW CONSULTANTS LTD, 9 REECE MEWS, LONDON SW7 3HE
Telephone: 071-584 2841 Fax: 071-589 9531 Telex: 297120 ERLOCO

West Tanfield, North Yorkshire
Deryck Hallam

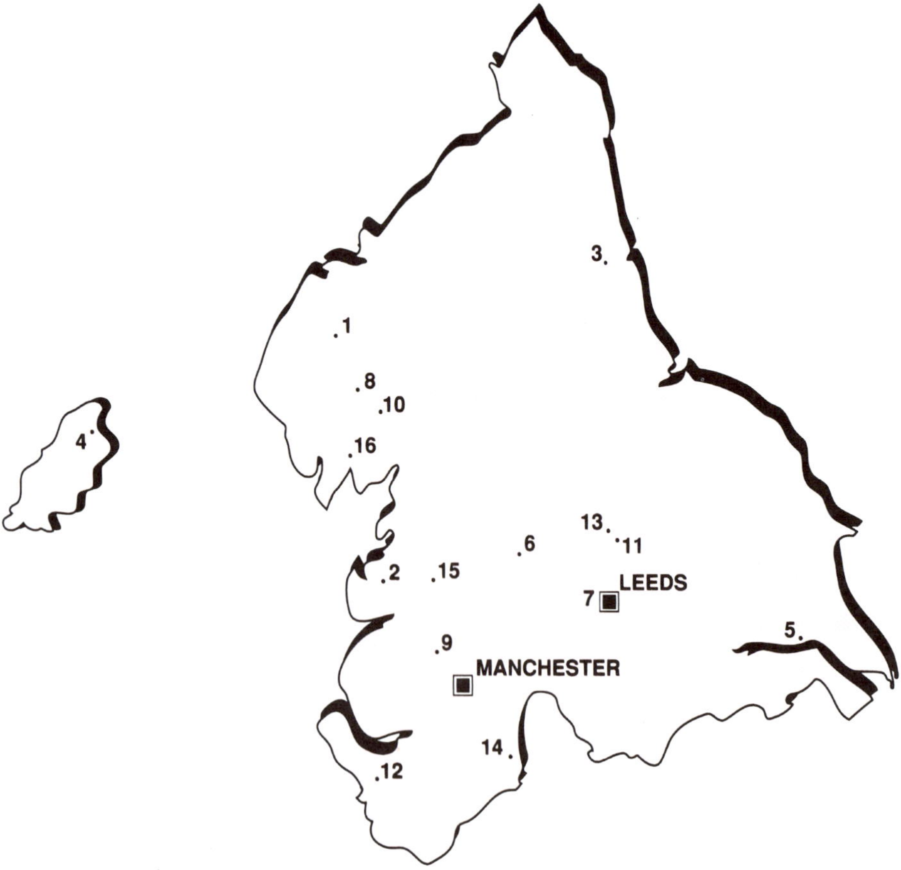
1
2
3
4
5
6
7
8
9
10
11
12
13
14
15
16
LEEDS
MANCHESTER

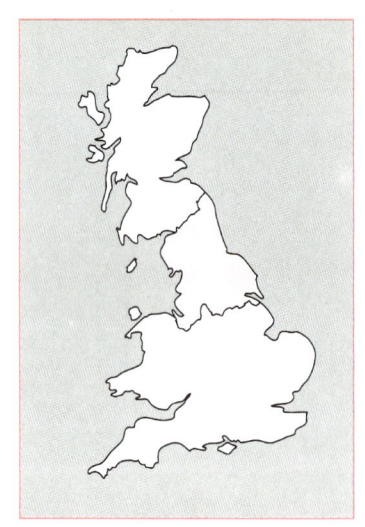

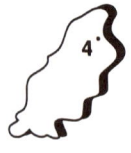

ESTABLISHMENTS IN NORTHERN ENGLAND

Map ref.		Page no.
1	Armathwaite Hall	152
2	Brooklands	154
3	Gosforth Swallow Hotel	156
4	Grand Hotel Isle of Man	158
5	Grange Park	160
6	Hartrigg Country House	162
7	Ladywood Lodge	164
8	Langdale Hotel	166
9	Last Drop Village	169
10	Low Wood	171
11	Majestic Hotel	174
12	Mollington Banastre	176
13	Nidd Hall	178
14	Shrigley Hall	180
15	Thorneyholme Hall	182
16	Whitewater Hotel	185

ENGLAND northern

ARMATHWAITE HALL
CUMBRIA

Armathwaite Hall Hotel
Bassenthwaite Lake   Keswick   Cumbria   CA12 4RE
☎ 07687 76551   Fx 07687 76220

42

Price category C

Armathwaite Hall enjoys a secluded situation in 133 acres of deer park and woodlands overlooking Lake Bassenthwaite in the heart of the Lake District.

Dating back to the Middle Ages and formerly a house of Benedictine nuns, it has been a hotel since 1930.

The Graves family, present owners since 1977, have skilfully modernised the hotel in keeping with its historic associations.

Public rooms are spacious and have wonderful fireplaces and wood panelling. Comfortable bedrooms have lakeside or parkland views, and modern amenities like en suite bathroom, television, in-house video, telephone hair drier and tea/coffee tray.

The wood panelled restaurant overlooks Bassenthwaite Lake and has a choice of table d'hôte and à la carte menus serving delicious 'Taste of Cumbria' dishes. Lighter meals, including high teas are served daily in the leisure club overlooking the swimming pool where the old coach house has been transformed into an attractive new area. Amenities include indoor heated swimming pool, jacuzzi, sauna, solarium, trimnasium and beauty salon.

Sporting opportunities at Armathwaite Hall are many and varied; tennis, pitch and putt, croquet, snooker, boating on the lake and hill walking in the Skiddaw Mountains. Armathwaite Hall has its own equestrian centre and offers riding and jumping tuition, country hacking, carriage driving, livery and riding holidays - prices on application.

Treatments

Treatments are available in the leisure club's new beauty salon run by Helen Marshall. These include Decleor holistic facials - the 5 Vitamin Aromatherapy Programme - £90 for 5 treatments or individually from £18 - £20; Triactive Aroma facial £40; skin-care make up £15; Seborreor facial £19; waxing from £3; manicure £7; pedicure £10; eyelash tint £6; back and shoulder massage to improve blood and lymphatic circulation £8.

Hairdressing from £5 shampoo and blow dry.

A £40 special day course includes sunbed, facial, back massage, manicure, pedicure and blow dry.

Tariff

Two night weekend breaks cost £128 per person in a standard room or £144 per person in an executive room - prices include dinner bed and breakfast for two nights.

Regular bed and breakfast tariff is from £98 for a standard room or £118 for an executive room (rooms accommodate two persons). Bed and breakfast rate for single occupancy is from £65.

Suites are available from £155 including one with its own battlemented turret and all-round views.

Travel Directions

Take M6 and exit at junction 40 signed Penrith, then A66 to Keswick roundabout. Take A591 towards Carlisle for 8 miles, turning left at Castle Inn junction, 200 yards from Armathwaite Hall.

Nearest railway stations Carlisle or Penrith, both 20 miles.

ENGLAND
northern

BROOKLANDS
LANCASHIRE

Brooklands Health Farm
Calder House Lane   Garstang   Preston   Lancashire   PR3 1QB
✆ 0995 605162

| 12 |

Price category B ✻

Brooklands is a small, well appointed health farm, situated on the edge of the Lake District in five acres of gardens. It offers residential courses of balanced health and beauty treatments, designed to rejuvenate and invigorate the body, and appealing to a mainly female clientele.

Amenities include heated indoor pool and spa bath, sauna, steam bath, sunbathing pavilion, solarium, conservatory room for exercising, jogging trail and tennis court. In the pool area there is a disabled changing room, shower and toilet.

Accommodation is in large, airy bedrooms appointed in Victorian style, most with bathroom en suite and all with television, telephone, electric blanket and tea/coffee making facilities. Recent renovations have provided six new ground floor en suite bedrooms and a lounge, while the refurbished East Lodge now accommodates four guests.

Choice of diet and treatments is discussed at the initial personal consultation - no detailed health or nutritional advice is given - although a local GP can be consulted.

When available, freshly picked fruit and vegetables from Brooklands' own kitchen garden are used. Meals as served plated, eliminating any temptation to cheat on portion size, and are taken in a somewhat austere dining room. Slimmers have daily menus of 1,000, 750 and 500 calories, and most dietary needs can be catered for if requested in advance.

Dressing for dinner is casual. Evenings are quiet with no organised entertainment or activities, allowing the opportunity to relax, catch up on correspondence or take some early nights.

Treatments

Body treatments:

These include body massage £12.50; G5 massage £10 or 5 for £45; panthermal bath £15; sunbed £3.50 sauna £8; Turkish bath £8; aromatherapy £12.65 to £25; reflexology £ 12.50; body scrub £10.50; waxing from £5.30; electrolysis from £5.75; Bio-Peel £19.

Beauty treatments:

Facials from £13.50; manicure and pedicure £10.00 each; waxing from £5.30; Cathiodermie £23; facial and make-up £21; eyelash dye £8, etc.

Hairdressing from £5 for a trim, £25 a perm, £7.75 for shampoo and set.

Tariff

A weekend break from Friday afternoon until Sunday afternoon costs from £220.30 single room or £214.32 per person sharing a twin bedded room. The tariff includes exercises, steam room and sauna, sunbed, body massage, facial and manicure on Saturday, and exercises, steam room and sauna, solarium, G5 massage and make-up on Sunday. The rates include all meals and use of facilities.

A *Full Day* costing £68 is available to non-residents and comprises optional morning exercises, sauna and steam room, swim, solarium, body massage, lunch, manicure facial and make-up.

Travel Directions

Take the M6 and exit at junction 32, taking A6 for 9 miles towards Lancaster. Turn onto B6430 at the junction and turn into Calder House Lane.

Nearest railway stations Preston 12 miles, Lancaster 12 miles.

ENGLAND northern

GOSFORTH PARK HOTEL
TYNE & WEAR

Gosforth Park Hotel
High Gosforth Park   Newcastle upon Tyne   Tyne & Wear   NE3 5HN
℡ 091 236 4111   (Fx) 091 236 8192

| 178 |

Price category D   A Swallow Hotel

This comfortable modern hotel on the outskirts of Newcastle has recently been acquired by Swallow Hotels. Set in 12 acres of wooded parkland, it boasts an excellent range of sporting and leisure facilities for visitors taking special Breakaway or Freedom breaks throughout the year.

The Gosforth Park Club's excellent facilities include an indoor swimming pool, sauna, steam room, plunge pool, whirlpool spa bath, solaria, games room and gym with computerised fitness assessment equipment. There are two squash courts, three all weather tennis courts, children's adventure playground and a 'trim trail' with specially designed obstacles.

Nominal charges are made for the squash courts and the sunbeds, but all other facilities are free.

Bedrooms are on three floors and are all comfortably furnished with private bathroom, hair drier, telephone, satellite television, mini-bar and bathrobes.

The hotel has two restaurants - the Brandling restaurant overlooking floodlit gardens or the less formal Vineyard restaurant. Pre-dinner drinks can be taken in any of the hotels' three bars, the Punters pub, the nautical Cabin Bar or the elegant Silver Ring cocktail bar. Afternoon teas are served in the relaxed setting of the reception lounge.

Treatments

The beauty and hairdressing salons are based in the leisure club and offer a full range of body and beauty treatments using Clarins products.

Body treatments:

These include Clarins Paris massage for the bust £24 or body £28; relaxing back massage using Clarins 'relax' oil £9; G5 massage £9.50 or 5 for £42.50; body massage £9 per 1/2 hour; slimming massage treatment to help eliminate fluid retention; £18 or 5 for £80; faradic toning session £10 per 1/2 hour or 5 for £45.

Beauty treatments:

All facials commence with skin analysis and conclude with a personal skin care programme for care of the skin at home. A deep relaxing massage to the face, neck and shoulder area is also included, making this beneficial to both sexes.

Paris facial massage £21; facials from £16; manicure £8; pedicure £10; waxing from £4.50; electrolysis from £7; eyelash tinting £6.

Complimentary consultations are available, and where possible appointments should be booked prior to arrival.

Tariff

One night bed and breakfast breaks cost £46 per person nightly.

Two night weekend breaks cost £120 per person and include dinner, bed and breakfast for two nights and one lunch.

All hotel residents have full use of the leisure facilities during their stay.

Travel Directions

Follow A1 until 5 miles north of Newcastle then turn onto A1056 to Wide Open.

Nearest railway station Newcastle Central 5 miles.

**ENGLAND
northern**

GRAND ISLAND HOTEL
ISLE OF MAN

The Grand Island Hotel
Ramsey   Isle of Man
☏ 0624 812455   Fx 0624 815291

54

Price category C

Perfectly situated, with palm fringed lawns sweeping down to the sea and panoramic views of the mountains and Ramsey Bay, this Georgian manor house has been renovated and transformed into a pleasant country house hotel with extensive health and leisure facilities. It is an ideal base for a short break or longer stay on this pleasant island with its many beautiful beaches, mountains and glens - all within a day's drive and worth exploring.

The comfortable bedrooms are individually designed in country house style with co-ordinating chintz furnishings. All rooms have en suite bathroom and a generous supply of quality toiletries. Baby listening devices enable parents to enjoy an evening meal with peace of mind.

Residents have a choice of restaurants - the elegant Bay Room overlooking the sea and offering a varied choice of à la carte and table d'hôte menus including freshly caught local fish, and the cheerful and informal Bistro.

Outside, there are no less than five croquet lawns (this is the headquarters of the Isle of Man Croquet Association) and a putting green. Access to golf courses on the island can be arranged on request.

Hotel residents have unlimited use of Grand Island's magnificent new Henley leisure spa with wave-swimming pool, jacuzzi, solarium, sauna, steam room, multi-gym, full size snooker table, hairdressing and beauty salons. Refreshments are available from the poolside bar.

Treatments

The highly qualified resident therapist Joy Phelan offers a varied range of treatments: Body massage - 1 hour £15 or £9.50 for 1/2 hour treatment - aromatherapy oils £2 extra; G5 massage £9.75; Sixtus foot treatment £11.50; faradic slimming treatments £7.75 each or 10 for £70; vacuum suction massage £9.50; manicure £6 - with paraffin wax £8; Ultradermie facial treatment £18.25; neck treatment £16.30 each or 4 for £49; Bio-Peel £13.50, etc.

Make-up, electrolysis and wax treatments are also available.

Top to Toe day packages are popular and include use of swimming pool, sauna or steam room, full body massage, facial and make up, manicure, shampoo and set or blow dry, morning coffee, salad lunch and afternoon tea - price £44.

Tariff

Accommodation is available in *Standard*, *Superior*, *Premier* and *Luxury* rooms and suites and starts at £54 single or £74 double room (two persons) for bed and full Manx breakfast.

A seven night bed and breakfast package costs from £192.50 per person.

Bargain two night weekend breaks cost from £39 per person are available in winter, and other packages featured all year except during late May and early June (TT Races).

Mylchreests Car Hire have a special package for Grand Island Hotel residents on short break holidays. A car can be hired at Douglas airport on a Thursday or Friday and returned to the airport by the following Monday evening. The charge for the hire including VAT is £47.

Travel Directions

From Douglas take the A2 road to Ramsey; the Grand Island Hotel is 1 mile north of Ramsey centre.

ENGLAND
northern

GRANGE PARK HOTEL
NORTH HUMBERSIDE

Grange Park Hotel
Willerby   Hull   North Humberside   HU10 6EA
☏ 0482 656488   Fx 0482 655848

109

Price category D

Grange Park is a country house hotel situated in landscaped gardens a couple of miles from the new Humber bridge and three miles from the delightful market town of Beverley with its 'perfect' minster.

The hotel offers good value leisure breaks which include use of the hotel's Tamarisk club with heated indoor swimming pool, steam room, sauna, whirlpool bath and solarium, as well as gym, hairdressing and beauty salon.

All bedrooms have en suite bathroom, satellite television, telephone, trouser press, hair drier and tea/coffee making facilities. Family rooms and rooms designed for disabled visitors are also available.

Guests have a choice of two distinctive restaurants, the elegant L'Eau Vive serving French cuisine or the more informal Cedars with Italian and English dishes. Quick bar meals can be taken in the Cedars Bar.

Treatments

Body treatments:

Aromatherapy massage full body £18, half body £9.50; muscle therapy full body £13.50, back and neck £8; G5 massage £8.50 for 1/2 hour; G5 spot reduction £30 for course of 10; full body paraffin wax £12, part paraffin wax £3.50.

Beauty treatments:

Although the range of treatments is limited, guests can take advantage of some unusual facials such as Mary Cohr Catiovital (described as the sister of Cathiodermie) which is very deep cleansing and costs £16.95. There is a DNA Facial Programme to rejuvenate and soften wrinkles £31.50, and a Geloide facial individually prepared £11.

Eyelash tinting is £4.50; eyelash extensions 'Tantaleyes' £9, renéwals 50p each; electrolysis from £4; waxing from £3; make-up £8.50; manicure from £5.30, pedicure £8.50.

Special health and beauty days can be booked in advance.

Total Performance (full day) costs £45 and includes sauna or steam, full body massage, Geloide facial, lunch, manicure, pedicure, shampoo and finish.

Prime Time (half day) costs £31 and includes back and neck muscle therapy, Geloide facial, manicure, pedicure, shampoo and finish.

The beauty therapists offer consultations without charge to discuss individual requirements.

Tariff

Special weekend breaks cost £85 per person and include accommodation in twin/double room for two nights, full English breakfast, table d'hôte dinner in L'Eau Vive on Friday, and dinner dance on Saturday.

When Sunday night is taken as a third night the cost is only £26 per person, including £11 meal allowance.

Travel Directions

From M62 motorway exit at junction 38 and take A63 towards Hull for approximately 5 miles. Turn left onto A164 Willerby road for 2 miles.

Nearest railway stations Hessle 2 miles, Hull 4 miles.

**ENGLAND
northern**

**HARTRIGG
NORTH YORKSHIRE**

Hartrigg Country House
Buckden   Skipton   North Yorkshire   BD23 5HA
☏   0756 760246

Price category D

Ladies' Pamper Weekends are a new type of short break for women of all ages, married or single, needing a change of routine, relaxation and a bit of well deserved cosseting. These popular spring and autumn breaks are offered on selected weekends by Longstaff Leisure from their Victorian country house hotel in the heart of the Yorkshire dales.

The weekends, hosted by Sylvia Longstaff and Laurence Earnshaw, start on Friday afternoons and continue until after Sunday lunch. Indulgences include tea in bed, farmhouse breakfasts, 'help yourself' lunches, home cooked evening meals with generous portions, candle-lit dinner on Saturday evening, and tea/coffee at any time.

19 guests can be accommodated in twin-bedded rooms and one triple bedded room (eight of the nine bedrooms have en suite showers and all have wash-basins). All rooms have stunning views of this remote and beautiful part of upper Wharfedale.

Full central heating and open fires in the two lounges (one with well-stocked bar) ensure warmth and a cosy atmosphere even in the depths of a Yorkshire winter (the B6160 road is accessible at all times even in bad weather.)

During the weekend a varied programme of healthy optional pursuits is organised:

Guided walks in this most picturesque part of the Yorkshire dales; swimming, sauna and jacuzzi at nearby luxury pool; use of exercise bike and rowing machine; musical relaxation hour; informal talks by various speakers on Saturday evening on topics such as graphology, fashion for everyday, etc.

Treatments

A resident beautician is on hand to provide a whole range of relaxing treatments:

Aromatherapy £18.50; facials £8.95 to £29.95; eyebrow and eyelash treatments £2.95 to £8.50; manicure/pedicure £4.95 and £7.95; body treatments from £11.95; depilatory waxing from £3.25.

Tariff

Cost of a healthy weekend with a difference at this friendly hotel is £95, with only drinks at the bar and beauty treatments charged extra.

Long weekends from Thursday afternoon to after lunch on Sunday cost £140 per person. Mid-week breaks Tuesday to Thursday have recently been introduced, these cost £95 per person.

Travel Directions

From Skipton follow B6265 to Grassington for approx 5 miles, turning onto B6160 at Thresfield. Hartrigg Country House is just before the village of Buckden.

Nearest railway station Skipton approx 12 miles (free collection).

ENGLAND northern

LADYWOOD LODGE
WEST YORKSHIRE

Ladywood Lodge
112 Street Lane   Leeds   West Yorkshire   LS8 2AL
✆   0532 731298

Price category E✳

Ladywood Lodge, a detached suburban house in a residential area of Leeds, has been turned into a natural study centre and retreat by homoeopath and aromatherapist Valerie Horsfall.

Operating since May 1990, the Lodge offers a wide range of mini and weekend breaks at reasonable prices with the emphasis on rejuvenation and healing.

Accommodation is in single, double or family rooms. Each room has tea-making facilities and television, and most have private facilities en suite. Ground floor accommodation is available on request.

Breakfast, lunch, evening meal and light supper are taken in the Lodge room - visitors can be assured that a warm 'Yorkshire' welcome includes plenty of delicious, wholesome, and mostly organic Yorkshire fare.

Amenities at the Lodge include sauna, solarium and jacuzzi, which are provided free of charge for visitors.

All guests should make a point of visiting nearby Roundhay Park's outstanding tropical gardens, aquarium and butterfly house. Admission is free and the gardens just a short walk from the Lodge.

Treatments

No beauty treatments here! Instead a fully qualified staff offer a range of alternative health treatments - aromatherapy, reflexology, psychotherapy, hypnotherapy, homoeopathy, crystal healing, meditation, relaxation, visualisation - all individually tailored to suit personal needs. Using one or more forms of alternative health treatments to accelerate body balance and aid healing processes.

Tariff

A choice of healthy breaks at Ladywood Lodge includes:

Rejuvenation week with daily relaxation, meditation and natural therapies £275 per person.

Rejuvenation mid-week break (three nights) with aromatherapy and clay treatment for muscle tone and weight loss £75.

Rejuvenation long weekend (Friday afternoon until Sunday teatime) with reflexology, aromatherapy and clay treatment for muscle tone and weight loss £95.

Ladywood Lodge also offers mini breaks called *Aspects of Healing* - designed to be educational, informative, entertaining and suitable for everyone. Held throughout the year and lasting from two to five days, they cover various topics of alternative medicine, and cost from £85 per person for a two night break.

One-day workshops on a wide range of subjects ranging from aromatherapy and relaxation, natural health and beauty for women, dreams, hypnotherapy, 'women who love too much', crystal healing, executive health, and many more. These cost from £4 to £15 per session.

Ladywood also runs a number of professional alternative medicine and therapy courses throughout the year. Full details on request.

Travel Directions

From end of M1 motorway (junction 47) follow A58 Wetherby road to Roundhay Park. Drive past park entrance and shopping parade on Street Lane. Ladywood Lodge is beyond the shops and petrol station, on the right hand side of the road.

Nearest railway station Leeds City 4 miles.

ENGLAND
northern

LANGDALE HOTEL
CUMBRIA

Langdale Hotel & Country Club
The Langdale Estate   Great Langdale   Ambleside   Cumbria   LA22 9JD
☎ 09667 302   Fx 09667 694

| 65 |

Price category C

This attractive hotel enjoys an exceptional setting in 35 acres of woodlands in the heart of the beautiful English Lake District. Nestling beneath the mysterious Langdale Pikes, the Langdale Hotel and Country Club is a self contained landscaped estate which won a Civic Trust Award for its outstanding contribution to the environment.

Main focal point of the hotel is the splendid Country Club. Hotel residents have full use of the outstanding amenities including heated indoor swimming pool, spa baths, jet stream exercise pool, sauna, steamroom, cold plunge pool, table tennis, supervised gym, snooker, games room and two squash courts. Outside are nature and trim trails, badminton, volley ball and an all weather tennis court.

Other active pursuits such as fitness and aquatone exercises, water skiing, rock climbing, guided mountain biking, mountaineering, guided fell walking, abseiling, windsurfing, horse-riding, etc can be arranged on request.

Children are well catered for too, with specially arranged activities such as fun and fitness sessions, family fun pursuits, adventure days, popmobility, craft, etc.

Hotel bedrooms are clustered village fashion in small groups, near to the main facilities. All rooms are double or twin-bedded with modern luxury bathrooms some with impulse shower.

Interior decor is either modern or elegant Edwardian with four poster or half-tester canopied beds. There are also a number of luxurious self-catering lodges available for weekly rental sleeping four to eight people.

Purdey's Restaurant has a great choice of international dishes and local cuisine. The tropical Tamarind Terrace overlooks the pool complex, where drinks and light meals can be taken.

Treatments

An excellent range of treatments can be enjoyed in the health and beauty salon:

Body treatments:

Body scrub and massage £21; back massage with infra-red treatment £12; body massage £13; G5 massage £13; body scrub £10; firming and toning bust treatment £10; Slendertone 40 mins £5 or 5 for £22; Clarins self-tanning treatment £14; sunbed 20 mins £5.50.

Beauty treatments:

Clarins facial £15.50; facial with bust treatment £23; day or evening make-up including a Pick-Me-Up Facial £15; manicure and pedicure £7.50 each or £9 each with paraffin wax treatment; waxing from £4; eyelash tint £5.

A *Three Hour Pamper* includes manicure, pedicure, facial and body massage and costs £40.

Hairdressing costs £6 for a shampoo and set, £6.50 for a wash and blow dry, and £4.50 for a La Maur conditioning treatment. Tinting, perming and colouring are also available at various prices on application.

Tariff

Leisure breaks include accommodation, full Cumbrian breakfast, newspaper, five course table d'hôte dinner and temporary membership of the Country Club and cost £66.50 per person per night sharing a room Sunday to Thursday or £76.50 per person per night sharing a room on a Friday or Saturday.

Single room supplement £30 per night.

Children under 3 are free of charge; under 14 years and sharing with 2 adults £15 per night including full breakfast.

Travel Directions
Take M6 and exit at junction 36 onto A591 by-passing Kendal. At Ambleside turn left onto A593. At Skelworth Bridge turn right onto B5343 to Langdale.

Nearest railway station Oxenholme (Kendal) approx 20 miles.

LAST DROP VILLAGE
LANCASHIRE

ENGLAND northern

The Last Drop Village
Bromley Cross   Bolton   Lancashire   BL7 9PZ
(C)   0204 591131   (Fx)   0204 54122

| 83 |

Price category C   A Rank Character Hotel

The Last Drop Village is an imaginatively restored collection of 18th century derelict farm buildings creating a whole new village in olde world style, with a pub, village bakery and tea-shop, weekly antique fairs, etc.

Village life revolves around the comfortable 83 bedroomed hotel with its unusual cobbled street leading from reception to the cocktail bar and two restaurants.

An outstanding leisure facility includes kidney-shaped swimming pool with wave pool, jacuzzi, separate saunas, four sunbeds, multi-gym, hairdressing and therapy clinic. Squash and snooker are also available.

All bedrooms have a choice of view, overlooking the courtyard or open countryside, and are complete with en suite bathroom, television, telephone tea/coffee making facilities, hair drier and trouser press. Luxury suites, some with four poster bed are also available.

Meals can be taken in the Stocks Restaurant or the unique Last Drop Restaurant, converted from the original cattle-shed and complete with original cow stalls and tables made from glass covered cartwheels.

Treatments

Health and beauty treatments include full body massage (ladies only) £14; back and neck massage £7.

Remedial massage, a variable treatment providing vigorous sports massage or gentler massage and movements for less agile persons costs £20 an hour; specific treatment massage for back, neck conditions, etc £15; general remedial massage for back, legs, abdomen or feet £12 per 1/2 hour (recommended for muscle, joint and circulation problems).

The beauty salon offers facials, depilatory, nail and make-up treatments, all at reasonable prices and bookable in advance or at reception.

Tariff

A two night weekend break which includes use of the leisure facilities (treatments and solarium extra) is £94 per person sharing a double/twin bedded room with en suite bathroom. This includes accommodation and dinner Friday, full breakfast and dinner dance on Saturday, and full breakfast on Sunday.

Single room supplement £10 per person for the weekend.

Travel Directions

From Motorways 61/62/63 and the M6, follow A666 towards Bolton and Blackburn turning right at the end of the motorway link. Turn onto B6472 signed Bromley Cross and the Last Drop Village is just a couple of minutes away and signposted.

Nearest railway stations Bromley Cross 1 miles, Bolton 5 miles.

* * * * *

The Last Drop Village is one of several Rank Character hotels offering short breaks combined with leisure and treatment facilities.

LOW WOOD HOTEL
CUMBRIA

ENGLAND northern

Low Wood Hotel
Windermere   Cumbria   LA23 lLP
ⓒ 05394 33338   Fx 05394 34072

96

Price category C   An English Lakes Hotel

The Low Wood Hotel has a relaxing ambience and lovely lakeside setting on the northern end of Lake Windermere, a short drive from the little town of Ambleside. The hotel itself has origins dating back 200 years, and boasts one of the most active leisure clubs in Lakeland.

All comfortable bedrooms have en suite bathroom, television, telephone and tea/coffee making facilities. Some rooms have beautiful lakeside views and four poster rooms are available.

A recent kitchen renovation ensures the provision of the best of traditional English cuisine, served in the Windermere restaurant. Morning coffee and afternoon tea are taken in the comfortable lounge, and pre-dinner drinks enjoyed in any one of four friendly hotel bars.

Hotel residents can enjoy a variety of activities in the new Low Wood Club, which is open to children at specified times. Additionally there is a supervised area for under fives and a games room with electronic and computer games for older children, allowing parents to enjoy the facilities of the club without distraction and with peace of mind.

Central focus of the Low Wood Club is the super pool area, imaginatively designed with cascading waterfalls, bubble bursts and tropical rain showers. There is a 50' stretch of clear water for serious exercising, and a separate toddlers' pool with its own fountains, shallow steps and beach!

Adjoining the main pool is the large jacuzzi, 'Roman Baths', sauna and steam rooms, power showers and an invigorating plunge pool. Other facilities include two solaria, two squash courts, table tennis, snooker, a well equipped gym with personally designed fitness programmes, and a health and beauty salon offering all the latest body and beauty therapies.

Treatments

Body treatments:

Decleor's relaxing and slimming treatments combine use of essential oils, plant serums and creams with a heating blanket - Aroma massage £25; Vital Harmony exfoliating treatment £18; Algoceane slimming and cellulite treatment £20; Aromatherm £20; Affinoderm £22 - all last an hour.

Slendertone £6 or 6 for £34; G5 massage £8 per 15 minutes or 6 for £44; leg care for poor circulation, varicose veins, water retention and poor circulation - includes essential oils and leg massage £12.50; anti-cellulite and stretch mark treatment using aromatherapy oils, packs and tonics £15.

The Health and Beauty Salon offers a variety of different types of massage to soothe tired muscles and promote well-being: Full body massage £16; back and neck £8; tension relief which includes a G5 massage to upper back £15; aromatherapy full body and facial massage 1 1/2 hours £25; aromatherapy body massage £20.

Beauty treatments:

Decleor of Paris products are used for a comprehensive choice of eight different facials from £20 each.

Other beauty treatments include light day make-up £15; skin care make-up artist facial £20; cleanse, tone and make-up £10; light day make-up £7; waxing from £3.50; electrolysis from £3.50; manicure with hand massage £6; pedicure including foot massage £10; eyelash tint £4.50; aromatherapy facial, massage, peel and mask £15.

Hotel residents are welcome to join in club activities such as circuit training, aerobics, exercise to music and aquarobics - full details and timetable at reception.

Other facilities:
The hotel has excellent on-site outdoor watersports facilities with its own water-ski school, tuition and equipment hire. Visitors who prefer a less strenuous way of enjoying Windermere can sail in Leander, the hotel's 32 foot steam yacht.

Tariff

A two night break sharing a twin or double room costs £60 per person per night Sunday to Thursday, and £65 per person per night Friday and Saturday.

Seven nights or more - £57 per person per night.

This short break tariff includes accommodation, full Lakeland breakfast and table d'hôte dinner.

Single room supplement £25 per room, four poster room £30 extra per night.

Children under 15 sharing parents' room pay only for breakfast and dinner.

Travel Directions

From M6 exit at junction 36 and take A591 signed to Windermere; Low Wood is 2 miles beyond the village.

Nearest railway station Windermere 3 miles.

ENGLAND
northern

MAJESTIC HOTEL
NORTH YORKSHIRE

The Majestic Hotel
Ripon Road   Harrogate   North Yorkshire   HG1 2HU
☏ 0423 568972   Fx 0423 502283

156

Price category C   A Forte Hotel

This truly grand Victorian hotel is situated amid 12 acres of gardens within walking distance of the town centre of this North Yorkshire resort. Orignally built in 1900 to accommodate visitors relaxing and bathing in Harrogate's therapeutic spa waters, the hotel has played host to royalty, the rich and the famous over the years. The spacious public rooms with their marble columns and gracious decor continue to be enjoyed by today's visitor, although sadly spa treatments are no longer carried out in Harrogate. The sulphuric waters can still be sampled in the town's Pump Room, reached via a short and pleasant walk through the hotel gardens.

All bedrooms at this opulent hotel are spacious and well decorated, with en suite bathroom and modern amenities.

Meals can be taken in the Edwardian restaurant which has an extensive menu choice and wine list, or in the many other restaurants and eating places of this elegant town - just a short walk from the Majestic.

Visitors to Harrogate can now use the magnificent municipal Turkish baths, which have been restored to their former glory and are now open seven days a week, with separate sessions for men and women. Details from the Majestic's front desk or the Tourist Information Centre.

The Majestic has its own Health and Fitness Club which boasts a large heated indoor swimming pool, saunas, solaria, spa pool, gym, snooker room, squash court and outdoor all-weather tennis court. Individual fitness assessments can be undertaken by arrangement and personal exercise programmes worked out.

Treatments

Karen Elizabeth runs the Majestic's Beau Monde beauty salon and offers body and beauty treatments with complimentary facial or body consultations.

Body treatments:

Treatments use an exclusive product range created at the GM Collin research laboratories in Paris and include Sudacho system body treatments for weight reduction £25; 6 treatment course for weight loss, health conditioning, detoxifying and combating stress £130; bust treatment £20; anti-cellulite or anti-stretch mark treatments £16 each; Swedish body massage £20; aromatherapy £35; body silk exfoliating massage £20; pre-holiday tanning massage £25; waxing from £4.

Beauty treatments:

Facials £18 to £25; eyelash tinting £10; manicure £8; pedicure £14. Karen also offers highly specialised Collagen 90 treatments - £60 per session or £250 for course of 5, and new Backscratchers nail tips £40 - allow two hours!

Tariff

Weekend leisure breaks at the Majestic which must include a Saturday night, are presently £59 per person per night in single or double room on a half board basis.

During the week the nightly tariff is for room only and is £80 single room or £95 twin-bedded room (two persons).

Travel Directions

From A1 take A661, A6055 or A61 signed to Harrogate.
Nearest railway station Harrogate 1/2 mile.

ENGLAND northern

MOLLINGTON BANASTRE HOTEL
CHESHIRE

Mollington Banastre Hotel
Parkgate Road   Chester   Cheshire   CH1 6NN
☏ 0244 851471   Fx 0244 851165

| 72 | ☆ | 🖊 | ♨ | ◉ | ⚒ | Kg | 📖 | ≋ | 🗡 | £ |

Price category D

Mollington Banastre is a country house hotel set in rural Cheshire just a couple of miles from the historic city of Chester.

The hotel offers a relaxing break with friendly service, good leisure facilities and appetising food from a choice of restaurants, combined with comfortable accommodation.

All rooms have en suite bathroom, television, mini bar, telephone and tea/coffee making facilities. Adjoining family bedrooms for children are available, some with bunk beds. Children sharing parents' room are accommodated free of charge. A number of four poster rooms and suites are also available.

Meals are served in a choice of restaurants; the Garden Room for formal dining with à la carte and fixed price menus, the Grillroom overlooking the swimming pool; the Terrace Bar for smorgasbord lunches, and the Good Intent - the hotel's own olde worlde pub in the grounds.

The Mollington Sportif is the hotel's leisure club with chlorine-free heated swimming pool surrounded by palm trees and exotic plants, special children's pool, jacuzzi, pulsating showers, sauna, squash courts, solarium, fully equipped and supervised gym with personalised health programme option, hairdressing and body/beauty therapies.

Treatments

A full range of treatments can be taken in the beauty salon, open seven days a week including:

Body treatments:

Massage £10; aromatherapy £25; faradic treatment £10 or £80 for 10; G5 massage £10; waxing from £4.

Beauty treatments:

René Guinot facials £16.50; Cathiodermie £18.50; Bio-Peel £16.50; eye treatment £14.50; eyelash tint £5; cleanse, tone and make-up £8; manicure £7; pedicure £7; electrolysis from £8.50.

Two comprehensive treatment packages are offered:

Top to Toe Treatment £55 - full body massage, Cathiodermie, half leg wax, manicure and pedicure, eyelash tint and eyebrow shape.

Hair and Beauty Special £50 - heat treatment or fast tan sunbed, full body massage, 1 hour facial to include cleanse, tone, steam, massage and mask, hairdressing consultation followed by a cut and blow dry.

Tariff

A popular feature of the hotel are the *Totally Whacked Weekends*. The visitor enjoys champagne breakfast in bed with free newspaper, full use of leisure facilities, soothing facial or relaxing body massage and £17.50 per person per day towards dinner in either restaurant
The cost of the two night stay is £135 per person.

Other short breaks are offered throughout the year at various rates - all include use of the leisure facilities.

The regular bed and breakfast tariff starts at £75 for a single room, £95 for a twin or double room and £107 for a family room.

Travel Directions

From M56 motorway exit at junction 16 and take A540 for 1 1/2 miles to Mollington.

Nearest railway station Chester approximately 2 miles

**ENGLAND
northern**

NIDD HALL
NORTH YORKSHIRE

Nidd Hall
Nidd   Harrogate   North Yorkshire   HG3 3BN
ⓒ 0423 771598   (Fx) 0423 770931

| 59 |

Price category B

This imposing 19th century manor house is situated in the heart of beautiful North Yorkshire amid 45 acres of peaceful gardens and parkland, just a few miles from the spa town of Harrogate.

There is a three acre lake stocked with mature rainbow trout as well as paths and trails through the delightful grounds which have extensive rosebeds and covered arbours.

Nidd Hall has a wealth of interesting architectural features - marble fireplaces, mahogany doors and fine wrought ironwork - all carefully preserved to enhance the Georgian ambience of this friendly country house hotel.

For the visitor seeking a healthy or relaxing break, Nidd Hall offers complimentary membership of the Leisure Club - amenities include indoor heated pool, squash court, all weather tennis courts, trimnasium, sauna, sunbeds, full size snooker table, games room with table tennis, hairdressing, beauty salon, poolside snack bar and boutique. Croquet, trout fishing and punting on the lake are also available.

The comfortable bedrooms are individually designed with colour co-ordinated furnishings and fine antiques blending with the Georgian flavour. All rooms have en suite bathroom, television, telephone, trouser press, hair drier, private bar and tea/coffee making facilities.

The culinary emphasis at Nidd Hall is on locally grown and purchased fresh fruit and vegetables. The kitchen gardens formerly covered eight acres, and will be restored to supply most of the fresh produce served in the hotel's two restaurants, the formal Lancaster, overlooking the terrace, and the Cellar, set in the vaulted 14th century cellars.

Most special diets can be catered for given advanced notice.

Treatments

Body and beauty treatments can be taken in the hair and beauty salon, and should preferably be booked in advance. The selection includes:

Back massage £10; full body massage £18, combined with G5 £20; faradic massage 6 for £43; manicure £6; pedicure £7.50; waxing from £2; eyelash tinting £4; facial with day make-up £16; full facial with massage £14.

Hairdressing services include perms from £20; highlights £14; conditioning treatment £9; blow dry £7; cut and blow dry £12; gentleman's cut and blow dry £6.50.

Tariff

Special two night breaks are offered at £75 nightly per person sharing a double room. This includes table d'hôte dinner (or equivalent from à la carte menu), full cooked breakfast, newspaper and membership of the leisure club.

Single room supplement £20 per night.

Travel Directions

From A1 take A59 to Knaresborough then B6165 to Ripley. The tiny hamlet of Nidd is about a mile from Ripley village. Travellers from Harrogate take A61 Ripon road for approximately 5 miles.

Nearest railway station Harrogate 5 miles.

ENGLAND northern

SHRIGLEY HALL
CHESHIRE

Shrigley Hall
Shrigley Park Pott Shrigley Nr Macclesfield Cheshire SK10 5SB
℡ 0625 575757   Fx 0625 573323

| 58 |

Price category C

Sited in the 260 acre estate of Shrigley Park in the pretty hamlet of Pott Shrigley, Shrigley Hall was restored to its former grandeur as an English country house in 1989, after 60 years as a Salesian monastery and college.

It is now a comfortable five crown hotel and country club, with exceptional health, leisure and sporting facilities, including an 18-hole golf course and a driving range.

All 58 comfortable bedrooms are individually furnished and decorated, have en suite bathroom, television, telephone, radio with alarm system, and tea/coffee making facilities. Many rooms enjoy extensive views over the estate.

The Cloisters and Oakridge restaurants serve a variety of different types of cuisine to cater for all tastes and appetites, and tasty vegetarian dishes are available. Dinner in the informal setting of the Cloisters costs around £10 to £15 per person. The more formal Oakridge restaurant's table d'hôte and à la carte menus start at £19.50.

Shrigley Hall has an unusual setting for its Leisure Club - it is housed in the former church building, and the extensive facilities include swimming and spa pools, sauna and steam room, solarium, hairdresser, beauty treatment room, snooker, two squash and two tennis courts and a fully equipped gymnasium expertly supervised, offering fitness testing and individual work-out programmes.

All facilities are free to residents with the exception of golf - green fees are £15 per round during the week and £22 at weekends.

Children under the age of 14 years are welcome to use the facilities but must be accompanied by an adult responsible for them.

Treatments
Body and beauty treatments available in the beauty salon of the Leisure Club include:

Full body massage £10; G5 massage £10 per 1/2 hour; aromatherapy - body and face - 2 hours £25; aromatherapy body only £20; facials £10 to £20; broken capillary treatments from £8; manicure £5.50 to £8.50; pedicure £6.50 to £8.50, etc.

Tariff
Weekend breaks cost £99 per person and include bed and breakfast on Friday and Saturday, dinner dance on Saturday night and use of the facilities (treatments extra).

The regular bed and breakfast tariff at Shrigley Hall is £85 per single room and £95 double room for two persons. Four poster rooms and suites are available - prices on application.

Travel Directions
Via motorway network to mid-point on A523 midway between Stockport and Macclesfield. Village of Pott Shrigley and Shrigley Hall are reached by an unclassified road 2 miles off A523.

Nearest railway station Macclesfield 6 miles.

ENGLAND
northern

THORNEYHOLME HALL
LANCASHIRE

Thorneyholme Hall Health Farm
Dunsop Bridge   Nr Clitheroe   Lancashire   BB7 3BB
℡   02008 271   Fx   02008 271

Price category B✻

Thorneyholme Hall Health Farm enjoys a remote and rugged location in the beautiful Vale of Bowland amid hills, forests and tumbling rivers.

Wendy Whitwell has converted this remote country house into a fine modern health farm, with a brand new wing and state of the art facilities.

Catering for only 38 resident guests at any one time, the emphasis is very much on individual needs.

All bedrooms are named after the different surrounding hills in the area, and are tastefully furnished with en suite bathroom and bathrobe provided for use in the health farm. All rooms have telephone, television and tea/coffee making facilities.

Shortly after arrival, visitors have a private consultation with experienced members of staff to arrange a diet and individual treatment programme from the wide range of body and beauty therapies available.

A generous number of treatments is included in the overall tariff - owner Wendy Whitwell maintains that everyone should leave the health farm feeling and looking their best, so a make-up and shampoo and blow dry is included prior to departure for all guests staying two nights or more.

Thorneyholme Hall opened in April 1991 so all amenities are brand new - these include heated indoor swimming pool, sauna, jacuzzi, steam room, solarium, hydrotherapy bath, gym, greenhouse relaxation centre, exercise studio and toning tables.

Exercise classes including step aerobics and aquarobics are held for all levels of fitness, and are included in the tariff, as are evening talks and demonstrations given on topics such as colour analysis, etc.

Outside facilities include an all weather tennis court, bicycles, croquet and putting greens. The surrounding countryside is ideal for walking, cycling and hill climbing - horse-riding, fishing and golf can be arranged.

Food is healthy and calorie counted, with the emphasis on fresh, raw and slimming menus. Individual dietary requirements are well looked after, with very light diets and 1000/1500 calorie diets available.

Treatments

Optional treatments are available and include facials from £12.50; cleanse, tone and make-up £9.50; manicure including hand and arm massage £8; Sixtus pedicure £12.50; waxing from £3.50; aromatherapy £25; exfoliation and skin softening treatment £12; slimming and firming treatment £17; firming and toning bust treatment £11; body massage £17; G5 massage £10; toning table session £8 or 10 for £65; sunbed £3 and £5; shampoo and blow dry £8.50.

Other treatments/therapies:

Lifestyle counselling £45 - 1 1/2 hours including computerised health assessment and work book; alignment therapy £25; stress/bereavement counselling £25; reflexology £25.

Various alternative health treatments can be arranged on request - these include iridology, colonic irrigation, homoeopathy, Bach flower remedies, naturopathy, nutritional counselling, osteopathy, phytology and acupuncture.

Tariff

3 day stay (two nights) from £316 to £335 single or £295 to £315 per person in a shared double room - rates include:

Consultation prior to treatments - 3 sauna, steam or jacuzzi, 3 massages, 3 sun beds, 3 exercise classes, 3 toning sessions, 1 facial, 1 manicure, 1 pedicure, 1 cleanse tone and make-up, 1 shampoo and blow dry.

5 day stay (four nights) from £530 to £575 single or £495 to £535 per person in a shared double room - rates include:

Consultation prior to treatments - 5 sauna, steam or jacuzzi, 5 massages, 5 sunbeds, 5 exercise classes, 5 toning sessions, 1 facial, 1 manicure, 1 pedicure, 1 cleanse, tone and make-up, 1 shampoo and blow dry.

Other rates for different lengths of stay on application.

A non-residential day including personal consultation, full range of body and beauty treatments plus hairdressing, with lunch and refreshments throughout the day is £75.

Travel Directions

From M6 exit at junction 31, taking A59 to Clitheroe, then B6478 to Newton. Turn left to Dunsop Bridge and along narrow road, Thorneyholme Hall is on left before entering village.

Nearest railway station Preston approximately 15 miles (transport to meet trains can be arranged).

WHITEWATER HOTEL
CUMBRIA

ENGLAND northern

Whitewater Hotel
The Lakeland Village   Newby Bridge   Ulverston   Cumbria   LA12 8PX
☏ 05395 31133   Fx 05395 31881

| 35 |

Price category C

Formerly a centuries old mill, Whitewater Hotel and the adjoining Cascades Health and Leisure Club are situated on both sides of the fast-flowing River Leven, the southern outlet of Lake Windermere.

Cascades was purpose built in 1984, and together with the hotel forms the Lakeland Village - an award winning leisure resort enjoying the driest and mildest climate in the Lake District.

Health and Leisure breaks are available throughout the year except on bank holidays with accommodation offered in single, double, twin, triple, or king-sized rooms (one with four poster bed). All rooms have a bathroom and shower en suite, and some have balconies overlooking the river.

Appointments for additional health, beauty and hairdressing treatments can be made in advance by telephone.

Day membership of the Cascades Health and Leisure Club according to availability is also offered to visitors in the locality and costs £10. This includes free sauna and towel and full use of club facilities - children's membership is £5 with no sauna provision.

A well-stocked boutique in the health spa sells a wide range of cosmetics, perfumes, leisure wear and everyday items.

Treatments

The many optional treatments include:

Aromatherapy, first treatment £42 (with bath and body oils for home use); steam cabinet and shower £5.50; moor peat bath £6.95; spa bath £5.50; body massage from £11 to £19.65; G5 massage £11; aromatic full body paraffin wax with heat treatment £19.20; 1 hour facials from £16; manicure and pedicure £15.30, etc.

Packages of treatments aptly called *Little Luxuries* can be reserved in advance like the *Tension Seeker* costing £21 with body massage, back paraffin wax, shower and infra-red treatment.

Non residents can enjoy a special health and beauty day £68, or a health and fitness day £28.50 which can be reserved in advance by telephone.

Tariff

The Health and Leisure Break costs £86.50 per night single or £146 per night double room (two persons) and is available for a minimum stay of two consecutive nights. The rate is inclusive of accommodation, breakfast and dinner in the hotel; morning coffee, lunch and afternoon tea in the Verandah Bar and the following treatments:

Daily heat treatment (steam cabinet, spa bath or sauna) and full body massage in Health and Beauty Spa, unlimited use of swimming pool, water exercise and fitness classes, whirlpool and exercise studio throughout the visit.

Travel Directions

From the M6 motorway exit at junction 36 and follow the A590 to Barrow. Follow through to Newby Bridge and dual carriageway, after which there is a sharp bend and the sign for the Lakeland Village - then turn right.

Nearest railway station Ulverston 8 miles.

Cader Idris, Snowdonia, Wales
Wales Tourist Board

WALES

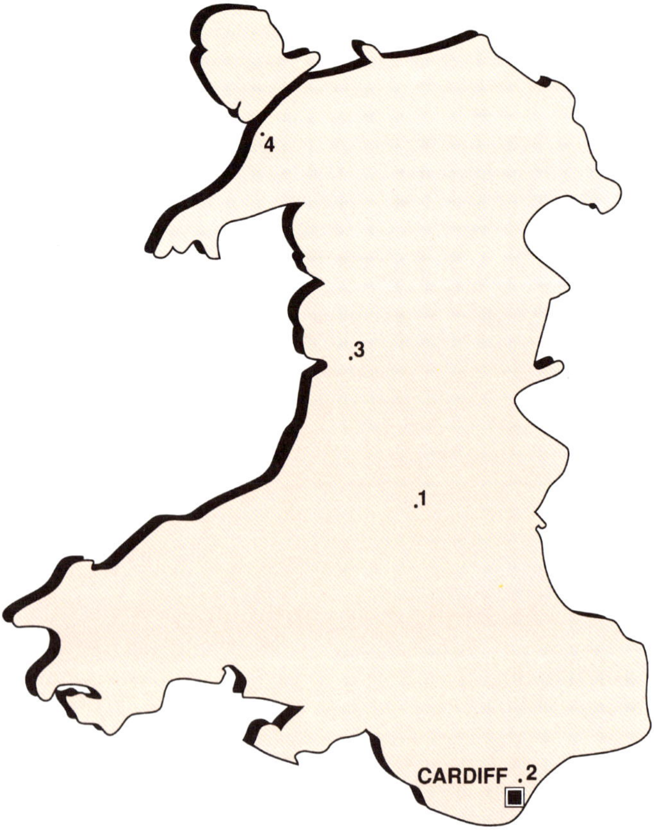

ESTABLISHMENTS IN WALES

Map ref.   *Page no.*

1. Metropole Hotel — 190
2. Miskin Manor — 192
3. Plas Talgarth Resort — 194
4. Seiont Manor — 196

WALES

THE METROPOLE
POWYS

The Metropole Hotel
Temple Street   Llandrindod Wells   Powys   LD1 5DY
☏ 0597 822881   (Fx) 0597 824828

121

Price category C

Revitalising two day breaks are offered at this family owned hotel in the charming spa town of Llandrindod Wells, where the town's Victorian pump room has been restored to its former glory, enabling visitors once again to sample the healing, mineral rich waters.

Surrounded by the beautiful Welsh countryside, the Metropole offers residents the extensive facilities of the Francis Leisure Complex which include a heated swimming pool, jacuzzi, sauna, steam room, solarium, bicycle and rowing machines - all housed in an attractive Victorian conservatory, in a constant temperature of 84°F.

Accommodation at this well-preserved Victorian hotel is on four floors serviced by two lifts. Bedrooms are decorated in soft pastel shades and have en suite bathroom, tea/coffee making facilities, television, hair drier, trouser press and telephone.

The Metropole has comfortable lounges and bars plus a first class dining room where salmon and trout from the Wye, Powys beef and Welsh lamb feature on menus complemented by fine wines.

Sporting and special interest breaks are offered at the Metropole throughout the year and include the *Revitalising Break* which incorporates a back/shoulder massage and facial with half board accommodation.

Treatments

A selection of body and beauty treatments is available in the Beauty Suite and includes:

1 hour's full body massage £14, 6 sessions of faradic massage £30, beauty peeling treatment £17, revitalising mini-facial £12; manicure £4.50; pedicure £5.75; eyelash tint £4; cleanse and make-up £5.50; waxing from £2.50; electrolysis from £4.

Tariff

The two night *Revitalising Break* costs £118 per person, and is inclusive of accommodation, two treatments, four course dinner, full breakfast and use of Francis Leisure Complex.

Travel Directions

Easily reached from M4, M5, M6, M50 and M54. Llandrindod Wells is situated on A483, 3 miles south of A44.

Nearest railway station Llandrindod Wells on Swansea to Shrewsbury line, just 350 yards from hotel.

WALES

MISKIN MANOR
MID GLAMORGAN

Miskin Manor
Miskin   Mid Glamorgan   CF7 8ND
☎ 0443 224204   Fx 0443 237606

| 35 |

Price category C   A Hidden Hotel

Although this lovely old manor house dates back to the llth century, its amenities and comforts are decidedly modern following a recent and total renovation and refurbishment.

Built of local stone and sited in 20 acres of gardens and woodlands on the banks of the River Ely, Miskin Manor is now a romantic and elegant country house hotel.

Hotel residents have temporary membership of Fredericks, the modern health and leisure club in the grounds, with free use of the swimming pool and gym. Other facilities in the club are available at nominal charges. These include three squash courts £1 or £2 per 1/2 hour, badminton court £2 per 1/2 hour, snooker table £2 per hour, sauna £3, solarium £2, spa bath £3, and steam room £3.

Gym tuition, aerobics classes, swimming lessons and yoga are held on a regular basis in the leisure club - see notice board for latest timetable.

All 35 bedrooms have en suite bathroom, television, trouser press, hair drier, and telephone, in addition to thoughtful extras like mineral water, fresh fruit and magazines.

Miskin Manor's attractive wood panelled restaurant serves high quality cuisine prepared from fresh local produce and complemented with an extensive wine list.

Treatments

Caroline Dore, therapist at the leisure club, offers a wide variety of body and beauty treatments at competitive rates.

Full body massage using nourishing body oils and lasting 1 1/4 hours £16.50; back massage £7; G5 massage £7 and £9; aromatherapy 1 1/2 hour body treatment including head and face massage and reflexology £20 (consultation free); Cathiodermie facial £18; Geloide Prescription facial £13.

Caroline also gives eye and neck treatments singly £13.50, or combined £25; manicure from £5; pedicure with foot massage £9.50; wax and electrolysis treatments from £5.50 with free consultation.

A relaxing *Top to Toe* treatment costs £40; lasting four hours it includes manicure, pedicure, full Cathiodermie facial and full body massage.

Tariff

Short breaks at Miskin Manor include accommodation, table d'hôte dinner and full cooked or continental breakfast, daily newspaper and temporary membership of the leisure club.

£225 for two people for two nights (third night £30 per person), or £122.50 for one person for 2 nights.

Short breaks are available any weekend except Christmas and New Year.

Travel Directions

Miskin Manor is easily accessible just 1/2 mile from Junction 34 of the M4, 8 miles from Cardiff.

Nearest mainline railway station Cardiff 8 miles.

WALES

PLAS TALGARTH
POWYS

Plas Talgarth Health & Leisure Club
Plas Talgarth Estate   Pennal   Nr Machynlleth   Powys   SY20 9JY
☏ 0654 791631   Fx 0654 791640

12 apartments, 63 lodges and villas
Self-catering basis   A Barratt International Resort

Plas Talgarth enjoys a superb situation in a corner of the Snowdonia National Park. This family health resort offers a wide range of health, beauty and sporting facilities centred around an ivy-covered Georgian mansion in 50 acres of beautifully landscaped gardens.

   Accommodation is in self-catering luxury holiday bungalows, villas and garden apartments, all centrally heated and fully equipped with modern appliances such as dishwashers, microwaves, food processors, crockery and cutlery. There is television with satellite stations, family games table, leather furniture, cocktail cabinet and selection of best selling books. Each villa has a private patio balcony or patio garden with wonderful views over the surrounding hills and mountains.

Indoors or out, a great range of facilities can be enjoyed at Plas Talgarth - all at nominal rates and sports equipment can be hired. There are indoor and outdoor pools, spa bath, solarium, steam room, sauna, squash and tennis courts, snooker tables, pitch and putt, children's play area, hairdressing and beauty salon and coffee shop. Plas Talgarth has bars and restaurants in which to enjoy good food in Welsh style - the 16th century farmhouse for lunch and the Dyfi View for dinner is recommended.

Treatments

Free consultations to discuss treatments are offered by the therapists - these include:

Aromatherapy £28 for first treatment and consultation lasting approximately 11/4 hours; reflexology or 'zone therapy' £18; steam cabinet £7; spa bath £7; full body paraffin wax £18; sun-tanning £2 to £6; various types of slimming massage treatments £9.50, and a wide range of face and body beauty treatments. Hairdressing for all the family is also available.

Tariff

Accommodation prices are per unit rental, and depend on number of bedrooms, type of accommodation and time of year.

Rates start at £175 per week in low season for a luxury studio sleeping two to four persons up to £335 for the same accommodation in high season.

De luxe lodges and apartments sleeping four, six or eight persons are available and range from £235 per week (four persons), £360 (six persons) and £385 (eight persons) in low season to £365, £585 and £605 respectively in high season.

Weekend breaks are also available throughout the year (excluding Christmas period) from £28 to £37 per person for two nights bed and breakfast and £33 to £47 per person for two nights dinner, bed and breakfast.

Travel Directions

Take M6 and exit at junction 11, then M54 and A5 bypassing Shrewsbury. Turn onto A458 Welshpool, then A470 and A489 to Machynlleth. Cross bridge and turn left onto road to Aberdyfi A493, continuing through Pennal - Plas Talgarth is on left.

Nearest railway station Machynlleth (London Paddington 41/2 hours).

WALES

SEIONT MANOR
GWYNEDD

Seiont Manor Hotel
Llanrug   Caernarfon   Gwynedd   LL55 2AQ
☎   0286 673366   Fx   0286 2840

| 28 |

Price category C

Seiont Manor is situated in some of the most beautiful countryside in Wales, close to Snowdonia and the Isle of Anglesey. Set in 80 acres of parkland with a salmon filled river running through the grounds, it offers peaceful relaxation with country house style ambience.

Leisure facilities are excellent - a large heated pool in a Victorian-style bath house, sauna, solarium, spa bath and invigorating needle shower, and well-equipped gym with weights to promote fitness and toning.

Every room at Seiont Manor is created round a different decorative theme, and is complete with en suite bathroom, tea/coffee making facilities, hair drier, trouser press, mini-bar, television and telephone.

Classic French cuisine as well as local Welsh dishes feature on the menus. The hotel prides itself on using only the finest fresh ingredients and even has its own extensive herb garden.

Treatments
Natural health body treatments in aromatherapy and reflexology are offered at Seiont Manor. Aromatherapy lasts an hour and costs £20 or £12 for 1/2 hour; reflexology is £12 per session.

Tariff
Special weekend rates are offered at Seiont Manor:

The rate per person sharing a twin or double room for dinner, bed and breakfast is £55 per night (minimum two night stay).

Book for four, five or six nights and the rate is £50 per person per night.

Stays of seven nights or longer cost £45 per person per night sharing twin or double room with dinner/bed and breakfast. Single room supplement £17.50.

Bank Holiday weekend tariffs are available on request.

Regular mid-week or single night tariff is £71.50 single or £97.50 double or twin (two persons) including full Welsh breakfast.

Travel Directions
Take A5 to Betws-y-Coed and Capel Curig and turn onto A4086 to Caernarfon, Llanrug is a few miles before Caernarfon.

Nearest railway station Bangor 9 miles.

SCOTLAND

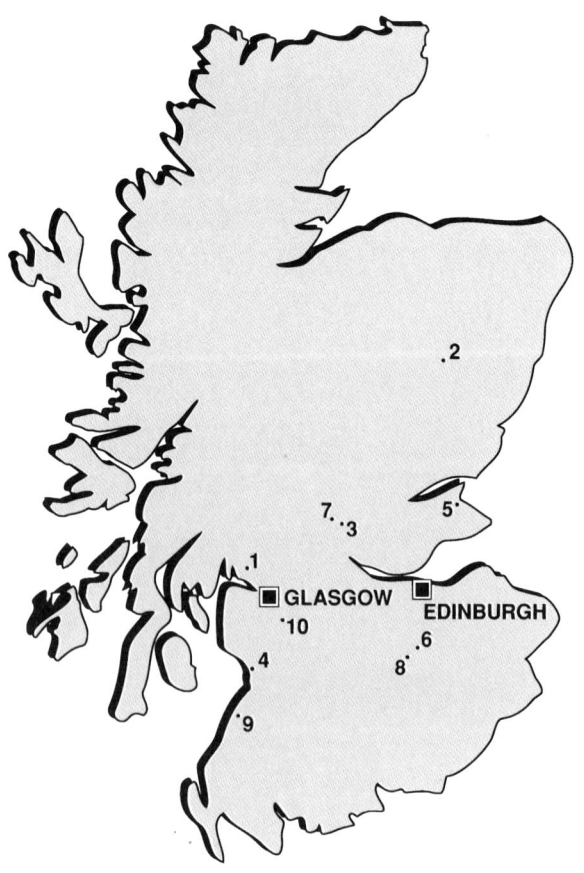

ESTABLISHMENTS IN SCOTLAND

Map ref.		Page no.
1	Cameron House	200
2	Craigendarroch	202
3	Gleneagles	204
4	Marine Highland	206
5	Old Course Hotel St Andrews	208
6	Peebles Health Hydro	211
7	Roundelwood	214
8	Stobo Castle	216
9	Turnberry Hotel	219
10	Westpoint Hotel	221

Goatfell, Isle of Arran
Alec Beattie

SCOTLAND

CAMERON HOUSE
DUNBARTONSHIRE

Cameron House & Country Estate
Loch Lomond   Alexandria   Dunbartonshire   G83 8QZ
(℅) 0389 55565   (Fx) 0389 59522

| 68 |

Price category B/A

With its 108 acres of lawns, woodlands and gardens sweeping down to the bonny banks of Loch Lomond, Cameron House must have one of the most romantic locations possible. Formerly an ancestral family home, it has been turned into a distinguished country house hotel with excellent health and leisure facilities.

Sports lovers can enjoy exercising whatever the weather (equipment can be borrowed) with two glass-walled squash courts, games room with table tennis and pool/snooker room. Outside are tennis courts with coaching available, a challenging 9-hole golf course (nominal charge), and sailing, cruising and windsurfing on Loch Lomond. Cameron House has its own marina and clubhouse.

All bedrooms at Cameron House have en suite bathroom, are tastefully furnished and decorated in soft colours, with television, telephone, tea/coffee making facilities, hair drier, complimentary sherry and fresh flowers. There are some specially designed family rooms with separate sleeping alcoves for children.

For garden enthusiasts, there is a Japanese water garden to explore, and acres of gardens with specimen trees and rhododendrons - and for the visitor looking for a new challenge, the climb to the top of Ben Lomond (973 metres) is rewarded with a magnificent view.

An excellent array of fresh Scottish produce including seafood from the fishing villages on the west coast, and locally grown vegetables and herbs is available in the hotel's three restaurants.

Among the many leisure amenities are two swimming pools (one, a fun pool with chute, the other a lagoon with waterfalls and rock pools), jacuzzi, sauna, steam rooms, high and low intensity sunbeds £6.50 and £5; fully equipped gym with professional instruction. Aerobic classes £2.50 and Callanetics £2 are held in the dance studio, which can also be used for badminton.

Treatments

Body treatments:

Aromatherapy body massage £25; body scrub and massage £21; contouring treatment £18; firming body treatment £18; exfoliating treatment £10, etc.

Beauty treatments:

Make-up including a cleanse tone and colour analysis £10; Clarins deep cleansing facial £18; desensitizing facial £18; and cosmetic camouflage lesson £6; manicure £10; pedicure £14; and waxing from £3.50. A full range of hairdressing services is also available.

Tariff

The nightly tariff includes full Scottish breakfast, complimentary newspaper and use of the leisure club and costs £102 single room or £128 double room (two persons).

Three luxury suites at Cameron House feature four poster bed, large sitting room and spa bath. These cost £245 per night (single or double occupancy) - extra adult £26 nightly, extra child £15 nightly.

Two standard suites cost £184 per night (single or double occupancy) with the same additional adult and child rates.

Travel Directions

From central Glasgow take A82 to Loch Lomond - a 30 minute drive. Cameron House is on the south west shore of the loch, 7 miles south of Luss. Turn right off the A82 at the sign for Duck Bay and the entrance is on the right.

Nearest railway station Balloch approximately 2 1/2 miles.

SCOTLAND

CRAIGENDARROCH HOTEL
ROYAL DEESIDE

Craigendarroch Hotel and Country Club
Braemar Road   Ballater   Royal Deeside   AB3 5XA
☏   03397 55858   Fx   03397 55447

| 50 |

Price category C/B

Once the Highland mansion of the Keiller 'marmalade' family of Dundee, this lovely country house hotel is set on a hillside in 29 acres of woodlands. It provides high class accommodation and excellent leisure activities amid picturesque Highland scenery - Balmoral Castle is just a short drive away.

All the bedrooms at this delightful hotel offer a high degree of comfort with en suite facilities, television, telephone, tea/coffee making facilities, hair drier and trouser press. Thoughtful extras provided include fresh flowers, books on local interest and even a trinket box with playing cards, sewing kit and other useful small items.

Three fine restaurants - the Oaks Gourmet Restaurant and the Lochnagar Restaurant in the hotel, and the Cafe Jardin in the Country Club - offer the very best of Scottish cuisine, with local game, beef salmon and trout featuring on the menus.

For vegetarians and those watching calorie intake, local vegetables and wholesome light meals are available.

All hotel residents have temporary membership of the Craigendarroch Country Club which has a comprehensive range of leisure and sporting amenities (enjoyed by Princess Diana during stays at Balmoral). There are two spectacular indoor pools, one an exotic lagoon with rock pool and waterfall, and the other a children's fun pool. Entry to the indoor pools complex is free to hotel residents, although some amenities and sports facilities have nominal charges: Squash £2 per 20 minutes; tennis £3 per hour; aerobics £4 per hour; skiing £6 per hour or £7.50 per 1 1/2 hours; solarium £6 per 20 minutes; snooker £3 per hour.

The Club has a spa pool, sauna, steam room, solarium, two squash courts, snooker room and fully equipped trimnasium. A pleasant crèche has been provided to enable parents with young children to enjoy a carefree visit to the Country Club.

Outdoor sports amenities include an all weather tennis court and a dry ski slope (with instruction) as well as countless delightful walks and trails through the estate.

Treatments

A luxurious health and beauty salon offers an extensive range of body, beauty and hair treatments for both sexes.

Body treatments:

Aromatherapy £25; body massage £18; body scrub and body massage £19.50; G5 body or back massage £6, etc.

Beauty treatments:

Clarins deep cleansing facial £14.50; Clarins reviving facial £8.50; manicure £8.50; pedicure £10; shampoo/set £6; wash/blow dry £7.

Tariff

The tariff includes full Scottish breakfast, newspaper and temporary membership of the Country Club and is from £87 for a single room, £118 for a double/twin for two persons.

Four poster rooms and suites are also available on request.

Travel Directions

From Perth or Aberdeen take the A93 to Ballater. Craigendarroch is just north of the village, and signposted.

Nearest railway station: Ballater 2 miles or Aberdeen 40 miles.

SCOTLAND

**GLENEAGLES
PERTHSHIRE**

Champneys The Health Spa
Gleneagles Hotel   Auchterarder   Perthshire   PH3 1NF
℡ 0764 62231   Fx 0764 62134

256

Price category A

Champneys Health Spa opened in January 1990 and is a collaboration between the famous health resort and Gleneagles, Scotland's most prestigious hotel, with unrivalled sporting and leisure facilities surrounded by some of Scotland's most beautiful scenery.

All accommodation at this unique Scottish institution is fully en suite, luxuriously furnished and equipped to the highest standards.

International and Scottish cuisine is served in the Strathearn Restaurant, and less formal meals can be taken in the Dormy House Grill or Country Club Brasserie.

Public rooms include a library and ballroom - with dancing to a resident orchestra most evenings.

The sporting facilities amid Gleneagles 750 acre estate are legendary, with the famous King's and Queen's golf courses, tennis courts, croquet lawns, jogging track, equestrian centre, clay pigeon shooting, and fishing.

Champneys Health Spa offers cosseted pampering in the most luxurious surroundings - aromatherapy, body and heat treatments (for men and women), facials and beauty treatments, can all be enjoyed here by hotel residents or members of the exclusive Gleneagles Country Club.

Treatments

Although some sporting facilities such as the swimming pool are included in the tariff, all health and beauty treatments are extra, full details in special tariff sheet. Amenities include:

Steam cabinet and spa bath £7; steam room or sauna £6; body massage £28 and £16; G5 massage £15; aromatherapy £38; manicure £10.50; pedicure £14; 1 hour Clarins facial from £23.50; high intensity sunbed £12 and £16.50; waxing from £5; make-up £12.50.

Tariff

Champneys Experience breaks cost £306 per person and include accommodation, breakfast and dinner for two nights. This rate also includes a personal consultation and four hours of different treatments in the Spa.

Regular single room rate is from £125 per night or £185 per night double/twin room with full Scottish breakfast.

Travel Directions

Gleneagles is easily reached on A9 Glasgow/Edinburgh to Perth road, turning onto A823 after Blackford.

Nearest railway stations Gleneagles 1/2 mile, Perth approximately 10 miles.

SCOTLAND

MARINE HIGHLAND HOTEL
AYRSHIRE

Marine Highland Hotel
Troon   Ayrshire   KA10 6HE
☎ 0292 314444   (Fx) 0292 316922

| 72 |

Price category C   A Scottish Highland Hotel

Breathtaking views across the Firth of Clyde towards the Isle of Arran are enjoyed by visitors to this friendly Victorian hotel, situated on the 18th fairway of the Royal Troon Championship golf course.

Over the last four years, the Marine Highland has undergone substantial modernisation and refurbishment, including the building of a splendid new leisure facility, the Marine Club. Hotel residents are entitled to make full use of the amenities which include large heated indoor swimming pool with jacuzzi, separate saunas, steam room, solaria, snooker room, two squash courts, beauty therapy room and fully equipped gym with personal fitness assessment facility.

All the Marine Highland's comfortable bedrooms have en suite bathroom and are furnished and decorated to a high standard. Rooms have television, free video system, hair drier, trouser press, telephone and tea/coffee making facilities.

Meals can be taken in either the elegant Fairways restaurant or the more informal Crosbie's which is open all day and until late at night with a good choice of food and a well-stocked bar.

Treatments

Marci's Beauty Room offers a wide choice of beauty treatments including some useful ones not always available in beauty salons, such as milia facial (removal of persistent whiteheads) £15.50; and removal of thread veins £12. Also available, Cathiodermie treatments from £18.50; mini-facials £8.50; cleanse and make-up £8; eyelash tint £5.25; waxing from £3.50; electrolysis from £5.50; manicure with hand and arm massage £6; pedicure with foot and ankle massage £7.95.

Body treatments which include a free consultation can be chosen from aromatherapy £18; Swedish body massage £18; skin purification for the back £13; back and shoulder massage £10; cellulite treatment £18.

For a special treat or as a gift, a 3 hour *Head to Toe* package can be booked. This consists of facial and make-up, manicure, pedicure, back and shoulder massage and costs £40.

Tariff

A full range of short breaks at reasonable rates is offered - all include full use of the Marine Club (treatments extra).

Weekend break - accommodation on Friday and Saturday, candle-lit dinner on Friday, full Scottish breakfast on Saturday and Sunday, dinner-dance on Saturday, traditional Sunday lunch. £118 per person October to May, £132 per person June to September.

Sunday Away break - Sunday lunch with carved joint of beef, afternoon tea, 5 course dinner, accommodation Sunday night, full Scottish breakfast Monday - £59 per person.

Short break - accommodation, dinner and full Scottish breakfast from £79 per person for one night, reducing to £59 per night for stays over two nights October to May or £66 per night June to September.

Golden Times (for over 60s) two nights or more - dinner, room and Scottish breakfast £49 per person per night April, May and October, or £56 per person per night June to September.

The regular tariff inclusive of accommodation and Scottish breakfast is £82 single room, £123 twin/double room.

Travel Directions

Easily reached via motorway network and A78 (follow signs to Prestwick airport), and turn onto A759 into the town of Troon.

Nearest railway station Troon less than 1 mile.

SCOTLAND

OLD COURSE HOTEL
FIFE

Old Course Hotel
St Andrews   Fife   KY16 9SP
   0334 74371   0334 77668

125

Price category A

Overlooking the 17th green of the Old Course, this famous golfing hotel has just reopened after a £15 million transformation. In addition to major structural improvements within the hotel, a brand new spa complex has been built, offering facilities and treatments on a par with those offered by the most sophisticated health farms in the UK.

All 125 newly renovated guest rooms including 17 suites, offer luxurious accommodation, marble bathrooms and every facility. Many rooms have balconies and French doors with views over the Old Course to the sea or towards the old town and the distant Scottish highlands.

Apart from golf and the 30 or so courses within the vicinity (this is the birthplace of the modern game), the surrounding area is a delight to explore, with art and antique shops in the old town of St Andrews, local castles, and picturesque little fishing villages.

There are no less than four restaurants in the hotel - all offering additional choices for the health conscious guest. Choose from the Road Hole Grill with its open kitchen and rotisserie, the formal Old Course restaurant, the Conservatory serving light meals throughout the day, or the Jigger Inn with real ale and wholesome food.

Hotel residents have free access to the Spa from 6.00am until 9.00pm, with treatments charged for as taken.

Facilities include a 50' lap pool and whirlpool in a glass conservatory, exercise room, separate ladies' and gents' steam rooms, sun tanning room, hair salon, juice bar and treatment rooms.

Treatments

Services and treatments include several alternative health treatments such as aromatherapy £31, shiatsu £26 and reflexology £18.50.

Body treatments:

The Spa has a choice of two wonderful wraps, which are preceded by a cup of herbal tea and a 10 minute session in the steam room. A salt exfoliating scrub is applied to remove dead cells, helping to make the body receptive to the properties of the wrap. A refreshing shower then follows before the treatment commences. Both wraps last an hour - the seaweed wrap costs £18.50 and the mud wrap £20.

Decleor specialised body treatments are also available from £27 to £41.

Beauty treatments:

Aromatherapy facials using pure natural plant products £26 to £40; make-up with lesson £10.50; eyelash dye £6.50; manicure from £7.50; pedicure from £10.50; depilatory treatments from £3.50, etc.

A full range of hairdressing services and treatments is available in the hair salon, with prices from £8.50 for shampoo and set or blow dry.

The *Day at the Spa* offers a day of relaxation and rejuvenation for men and women costing £70.50. This includes consultation with a qualified therapist to advise on treatments, unlimited use of spa facilities, aquarobics class, wrap with body scrub or full body massage and manicure, sunbed, facial and spa lunch.

Half days of health and beauty are also available for £36.

Tariff

Residential *Body and Soul* breaks for a minimum of two nights cost from £127.50 to £137 per night per person. This rate includes dinner, bed and breakfast and the following treatments in the Spa:

Two sunbed sessions, one aromatherapy massage, one Swedish massage, facial, manicure, hair wash and blow dry.

Accompanying partners can have a round of golf instead of the treatments if they prefer, with full use of the Spa facilities during their visit.

Lifestyle two night breaks are also offered - the break includes dinner, bed and breakfast and costs from £86 to £96 per person per night sharing a double room.

Regular room only tariff is from £123 per night single occupancy to £159 double occupancy. Breakfast is £10.50 per person.

Travel Directions

St Andrews is reached by the Forth Bridge and M90 from Edinburgh. Exit the motorway at junction 8 and take A91 to St Andrews. From Glasgow take M80 exiting at junction 9 and taking A91 to St Andrews.

Nearest railway station Leuchars 5 miles.

PEEBLES HOTEL HYDRO
PEEBLESSHIRE

SCOTLAND

Peebles Hotel Hydro
Innerleithen Road   Peebles   Peeblesshire   EH45 8LX
☏ 0721 20602   Fx 0721 22999

|135|

Price category D/C

Nestling in the heart of the beautiful Scottish Borders in 30 acres of grounds, the Peebles Hydro Hotel is a complete resort in its own right, offering an extensive range of holiday packages all year round. Privately owned, the Hydro opened in 1907 and still retains a comfortable Edwardian atmosphere alongside modern comforts and amenities.

A wide range of accommodation is offered including family rooms, suites and superior twin rooms with balconies.

All bedrooms have en suite bathroom, trouser press, hair drier, television and tea/coffee making facilities.

The dining room overlooks the Tweed valley and offers a varied menu of haute cuisine and traditional Scottish dishes prepared with fresh local produce. For slimmers and vegetarians 'Healthier eating' dishes are available daily.

This is an ideal hotel for family holidays, as children are welcomed and enjoy most of the splendid facilities as well as weekly sports and games programmes during the summer months. Dances and discos are held at weekends in the hotel ballroom, with occasional fancy dress parties and teenage discos

As a 'resort' hotel, the Hydro provides a full range of indoor recreation facilities, with badminton, squash courts, table tennis and snooker tables, as well as the Bubbles leisure complex with heated swimming pool, sauna, solarium, steam bath and gym.

Outside are tennis courts, croquet, putting, pitch and putt, pony-trekking, and an adventure playground. A 20% discount on rounds of golf played over Peebles Course is offered to hotel residents, tickets available from reception.

Treatments

A wide range of body and beauty treatments can be enjoyed in the beauty salon. Beauty therapist Jackie Anderson uses an exclusive range of Elemis products in her treatments.

Body treatments:

Aromatherapy £18; faradic muscle toning machine course of 3 sessions £18, 6 sessions £31, 10 sessions £48; G5 massage £6 for 1/2 hour, 6 for £30; waxing and electrolysis from £3 to £16.

Beauty treatments:

Deep cleansing facials with face and shoulder massage £13; face mask and ozone steaming £12; facial as above with facial peel £13; aromatherapy facial with pressure point face and shoulder massage using aromatic oils and face mask £12; manicure and pedicure with massage £7 and £8; eyelash tinting £5.50; make-up lesson £12.

Special morning or afternoon treatment packages can be booked and cost £50 - these incorporate leg wax with bikini line, underarm wax, eyebrow trim and lash tint, manicure and pedicure, facial with massage, face mask and ozone steaming and make-up.

A *Soothing Experience* costs £35 and includes full body massage, facial with massage, face mask and ozone cleaning, manicure and pedicure.

Tariff

Price of accommodation depends on time of year, number of nights stayed and type of room required.

The price per person per night for a two night stay in a standard twin-bedded room is £43.23 October to March, £47.25 April to June, £53.25 June to mid-August, £49.25 late August to October and £45.25 October to mid-December.

The price includes accommodation, full breakfast and table d'hôte dinner. A superior twin bedroom with balcony for 2 nights costs from £48.25 per person per night and a suite £62.

There is a complicated table of modest charges for children, dependent on age, length of stay, time of year, etc, prices on application.

Pamper Yourself Breaks are available - throughout the year at various rates which include half board accommodation and use of health facilities (nominal charge for solarium, snooker and squash). Extra charge for superior bedroom with front view.

Travel Directions

Peebles is in the Scottish Border country, 22 miles from Edinburgh and 55 miles from Glasgow. It is on A72 approximately 16 miles from Galashiels.

Nearest railway station Edinburgh Waverley 22 miles.

SCOTLAND

ROUNDELWOOD
TAYSIDE

Roundelwood Health and Fitness Centre
Drummond Terrace   Crieff   Tayside   PH7 4DG
☏   0764 3806

| 7 | ☆ | 🦱 | ≋ | ◉ | ✂ | ⚖ | ✕ | ✗ | ☺ | 🍇 | 🐟 | 🔍 | 🏃 |

Price category D✻

Roundelwood has the advantage of being situated amid some of the loveliest Scottish scenery, with many famous beauty spots close at hand. It overlooks the picturesque town of Crieff, known as the 'Gateway to the Highlands', an attractive holiday town worth exploring.

Popular health, fitness and slimming courses are held throughout the year for up to ten participants. These include weight control, stress management and relaxation programmes, stop smoking therapy, as well as physiotherapy for all back, joint and muscular problems.

Simple tests are carried out initially to ascertain ideal weight and overall fitness goals. A course supervisor then arranges treatments accordingly. Visitors have unlimited use of sauna, solarium, sunbed, hydrotherapy pool, fully equipped gym and nearby swimming pool facilities - Roundelwood does not have its own pool for swimming. The tariff also covers face and skin care and an appointment with the hairdresser prior to departure.

Optional outdoor activities are arranged each day and include guided hill walks and cycle rides - so appropriate clothing and strong shoes for walking are essential. A minibus operates according to demand, taking guests on afternoon trips to such lovely spots as Loch Earn, Glen Lednock and the Sma' Glen.

For the first day or so, fruit and salad meals only are served, followed by a balanced wholefood vegetarian diet using vegetables and fruit from Roundelwood's own kitchen garden whenever possible. Meals are served in the rooftop dining room with splendid views over the Grampian Mountains.

All bedrooms have en suite facilities. There is a lift to all floors, two lounges and a dining room as well as a sun roof and lounge.

Roundelwood provides a nursing care service for convalescing patients after surgery or illness, and a number of rooms are used for this purpose, but kept seperate from the health courses.

Treatments

The *Health and Fitness* course offers a complete package of treatments from Monday to Friday, including aromatherapy, massage, sauna, solarium, spa bath, sunbed, Slendertone, G5 massage and thermal wraps.

Optional treatments can be taken if desired, although the range of inclusive treatments is comprehensive - an extra G5 or Slendertone costs £4; eyelash tint £4; waxing from £3; manicure £5.50. A special beauty package can be booked for £12 and includes two facials, a shampoo and set or blow dry.

Tariff

Five days is the minimum length of stay at Roundelwood, but the 12 day course is recommended. All courses begin on a Sunday evening and finish after lunch on Friday - visitors staying for the 12 day course stay free of charge on the weekend. No treatments are given on Saturdays or Sundays.

A single room with en suite bathroom is £295 for five nights or £590 for a 12 night stay. Sharing a twin-bedded room with en suite bathroom is £242 per person for five nights, or £483 for 12 nights.

The tariff includes accommodation, treatments and all meals.

Travel Directions

Take the M9 and exit at junction 9, taking A9 and then either A822 or A823 to Crieff. Follow A85 signed to Comrie, Lochearnhead or Crianlarich to the edge of the town. Follow signs to Roundelwood.

Nearest railway station Gleneagles 11 miles.

SCOTLAND

STOBO CASTLE
PEEBLESSHIRE

Stobo Castle Health Spa
Stobo Castle   Peeblesshire   EH45 8NY
℡ 07216 249   Fx 07216 294

| 19 |

Price category B✳

If living in a lovely old Scottish castle appeals, then Stobo Castle Health Spa in the beautiful Peeblesshire countryside makes an ideal choice.

Purchased by the Winyard family in 1978 and skilfully transformed into a modern health resort, Stobo Castle has a warm and friendly atmosphere despite the grandeur of its palatial decor and furnishings.

The spa area is cosily tucked away in the basement of the castle - past suits of armour and down a warm maze of carpeted corridors and treatment rooms. Programmes are based on weekly, five night or two night weekend periods.

All bedrooms are individually designed and furnished and most have en suite facilities - all have telephone and television. Although the castle is beautifully warm, all beds are provided with electric overblankets for extra comfort.

A cosy log fire creates a homely and friendly atmosphere in the lounge, and is especially welcome on chilly winter evenings,

Meals are nutritious, well presented and calorie counted to make dieting easy and pleasurable. 400, 800 and 1,000 calorie diets are available and surprisingly satisfying - there is always a good choice of vegetarian options. Non-dieting guests can take full advantage of the delicious and plentiful array of healthy wholefood dishes - which should satisfy the most demanding of appetites. Most of Stobo's larder is stocked with produce from local farms - beef, lamb, Scottish salmon and game. Even the water supply is special - it is piped - pure and sparkling from Stobo's own spring.

Breakfast is served buffet style in the elegant wood-panelled dining room (or in bed if preferred), followed by a three course lunch and a satisfying dinner in the evening, after which an exquisite Japanese water garden complete with waterfalls invites exploration, as well as many other pleasant walks in the area.

The atmosphere at Stobo is totally informal - there is no need to dress up - track suits and dressing gowns are acceptable attire throughout the day and evening, and for those who come unprepared, there is a boutique selling a selection of casual wear.

Easy exercise classes and dance therapy are held regularly, together with relaxation and self defence classes. Other recreational activities include a small heated indoor exercise pool, whirlpool, tennis and cycling. Enjoyable and vigorous conducted walks are also organised.

Treatments

The number of inclusive treatments is based on the actual number of nights in residence, and includes body massage by hand, vibro or underwater; Slendertone; sunbed or infra-red, and heat treatments such as sauna, steam and spa baths.

Stobo Castle's extensive choice of optional health and beauty treatments should preferably be reserved at the time of booking.

Body treatments:

Sauna or steam cabinet £8.50; spa bath £8.50; Slendertone £12.50; Cathiodermie £26; aromatherapy £35; reflexology £19.50; Ionithermie £33; heavy legs treatment with Thalgo plasma gel £11; sunbed £8.50.

An Acu-massager machine is a new optional treatment, giving oriental shiatsu-type massage to 55 acupressure points in the neck, shoulders, back, thighs and calf muscles. Two integrated heaters soothe sore back muscles with penetrating warmth. The treatment takes 25 minutes and costs £14.

Beauty treatments:
Cathiodermie £26; manicure £14.50 or £11.50 (men's); Sixtus pedicure £16.50 or £13.50 (men's); eyelash dye £9.50; waxing from £5.50; make-up lesson £20; shampoo and conditioner £5; shampoo and blow dry or set £11.50; trim and blow dry for men £10; trim and blow dry ladies £15.

Tariff
A *Health and Beauty* or *Health and Fitness* stay (eight or nine treatments over two night stay) starts at £108 per person per night in a twin-bedded room or £115 in a single room with vanity unit. En suite accommodation from £135 single or £116 per person sharing a twin or double room.

A *Holiday Plan* (four treatments over a two night stay) is £88 per person per night in a twin-bedded room or £99 in a single room with vanity unit. En suite accommodation from £96 per person in a twin or double room or £120 in a single room.

Please note, the above rates DO NOT include VAT, which is added to all accounts at the current rate.

Travel Directions
From Glasgow and Edinburgh head for the A72 to Peebles then B712 directly to the village of Stobo. Travellers from the south take either A74, A68 or A1 into the Borders, then A72 and B712.

Nearest railway station Edinburgh Waverley 27 miles.

TURNBERRY HOTEL
AYRSHIRE

SCOTLAND

Turnberry Hotel
Turnberry   Ayrshire   KA26 9LT
ⓒ 0655 31000   (Fx) 0655 31706

|132|

Price category A

The tiny village of Turnberry on the Firth of Clyde is famous for its splendid hotel and two championship golf courses which attract visitors from all over the world.

Millions have already been spent upgrading and refurbishing this fine Edwardian hotel to the highest international standards. In 1991, a £6 million spa complex was added to the hotel's amenities, incorporating Scotland's first ever thalassotherapy suite. The new complex has a spectacular sea view, 20 metre swimming pool and spa pool, children's pool, sauna, bio sauna, steam rooms, plunge pool, body showers and relaxation areas. There is also a restaurant and bar, solarium, squash court and gym as well as treatment rooms and beauty salon with ladies' and gentlemen's hairdressing. New luxury accommodation and a restaurant complete the complex which is accessible by lifts from the main hotel building.

Turnberry's bedrooms are individually designed with lovely colour schemes and furnishings, and many have wonderful views over the golf course to the sea and distant mountains of the Isle of Arran. All have spacious en suite bathroom with bath and shower, bathrobes, hair drier, television and telephone.

Many other leisure pursuits can be enjoyed at Turnberry apart from golf on the famous links - pitch and putt, croquet, tennis, horse riding, swimming, fishing and billiards. There are deserted sandy beaches, pretty villages, towns and many places of interest to visit in the area - Culzean Castle, Croy Bay, Ayr and Robbie Burns country, even the islands of Arran, Millport and Ailsa Craig can be reached in a day's outing.

Treatments

Body, beauty and a range of 25 thalassotherapy treatments are available in the Spa and can be reserved in advance.

Body treatments:

Lifestyle and fitness evaluation £50; cholesterol check £15; aromatherapy £35; body massage £25; hydrotherapy massage bath with essential oils £30; total body mask with algae, mineral salts or Dead Sea Mud for detoxifying £30; body blitz to boost circulation £16, etc.

Beauty treatments:

Turnberry facial £25; manicure £20; pedicure £20; ultra pampering facial £50, etc.

Tariff

Four residential packages are offered - *Health and Fitness, Anti-Stress, Hydrotherapy* and *Luxury Pampering* - all include several treatments and full use of Spa, exercise, fitness and sports facilities.

The Spa packages include accommodation and Scottish or light breakfast and cost £264 per person sharing a double room for two nights or £630 per person sharing a double room for five nights.

Several day guest programmes are available from £85 per person. All include various treatments and a light lunch in the Bay at Turnberry Restaurant.

Regular bed and breakfast tariff costs from £115 per person per night.

Travel Directions

The A77 Glasgow to Stranraer road passes within half a mile of the hotel. Glasgow airport is 55 miles from Turnberry.

Nearest railway station Girvan 6 miles.

WESTPOINT HOTEL
STRATHCLYDE

SCOTLAND

Westpoint Hotel
Stewartfield Way Philipshill East Kilbride Strathclyde G74 5LA
☏ 03552 36300   Fx 03552 33552

| 74 |

Price category C

Situated in quiet landscaped gardens on the outskirts of East Kilbride, 20 minutes from central Glasgow, Westpoint Hotel is the brand new sister hotel to Scottish resort hotels Craigendarroch and Cameron House.

The luxury hotel and country club opened in May 1991, and offers visitors superb accommodation, high-class cuisine and leisure facilities.

The modern bedrooms are comfortable and luxurious having full en suite bathroom, satellite television, telephone, tea/coffee making facilities, use of bathrobes and welcoming sherry.

All the public rooms of this contemporary hotel are situated on the ground floor, overlooking the gardens creating a pleasant, almost countryside atmosphere.

Breakfast, lunch and dinner are taken in the informal setting of the Point Grill, where there are à la carte and table d'hôte menus, with daily vegetarian choices. Pre-dinner drinks and snacks are served in the Points lounge bar from noon onwards.

In the evenings, guests can dine in the hotel's gourmet restaurant 'Simpson's' which is rapidly becoming well known for its excellent formal cuisine. A five course table d'hôte dinner with coffee presently costs £38.50. The restaurant is open for dinner only - Monday to Saturday.

Westpoint Hotel's leisure facilities are truly outstanding - all hotel residents have temporary membership of The Club, the hotel's superb private country club.

Facilities include a magnificent indoor pool complex with large heated pool, children's fun pool, poolside spa bath, sauna, steam room and plunge pool. 'Dry' amenities include dance studio, solarium, supervised crèche, snooker room with two full-sized championship tables, and a health and beauty salon using Clarins products.

Treatments

Body treatments:

Clarins bust treatment £18; firming body treatment £20; 1 hour relaxing massage £20; back massage £12; sunbed - 30 minutes £10, 15 minutes £5; aromatherapy massage £28; aromatherapy facial £15; aromatherapy back massage £18; Paris Method treatments from £22.

Beauty treatments:

Clarins facials £14 to £20; make-up (with cleanse, tone and colour analysis) £10; eyebrow and eyelash tinting from £4; waxing £4; manicure £10; pedicure £15; exfoliation and self-tanning treatment £35.

Treatments for men:

Back and shoulder massage £12; one hour body massage £20; men's facial £18; aromatherapy back massage £18; aromatherapy body massage £28; manicure £8 and pedicure £12.

Tariff

A special weekend rate of £52.50 per person per night sharing a double room applies to accommodation reserved for two nights on Friday, Saturday and Sunday nights. These rates include dinner bed and breakfast and full use of leisure facilities.

Single supplement £20 per night.

Regular bed and breakfast tariff is £85 single and £105 double (two persons).

Travel Directions

From M74 take exit 6 and follow signs to Hamilton and East Kilbride. Nearest railway station Glasgow Central approximately 6 miles.

Lakes of Killarney, Co. Kerry
Irish Tourist Board

IRELAND

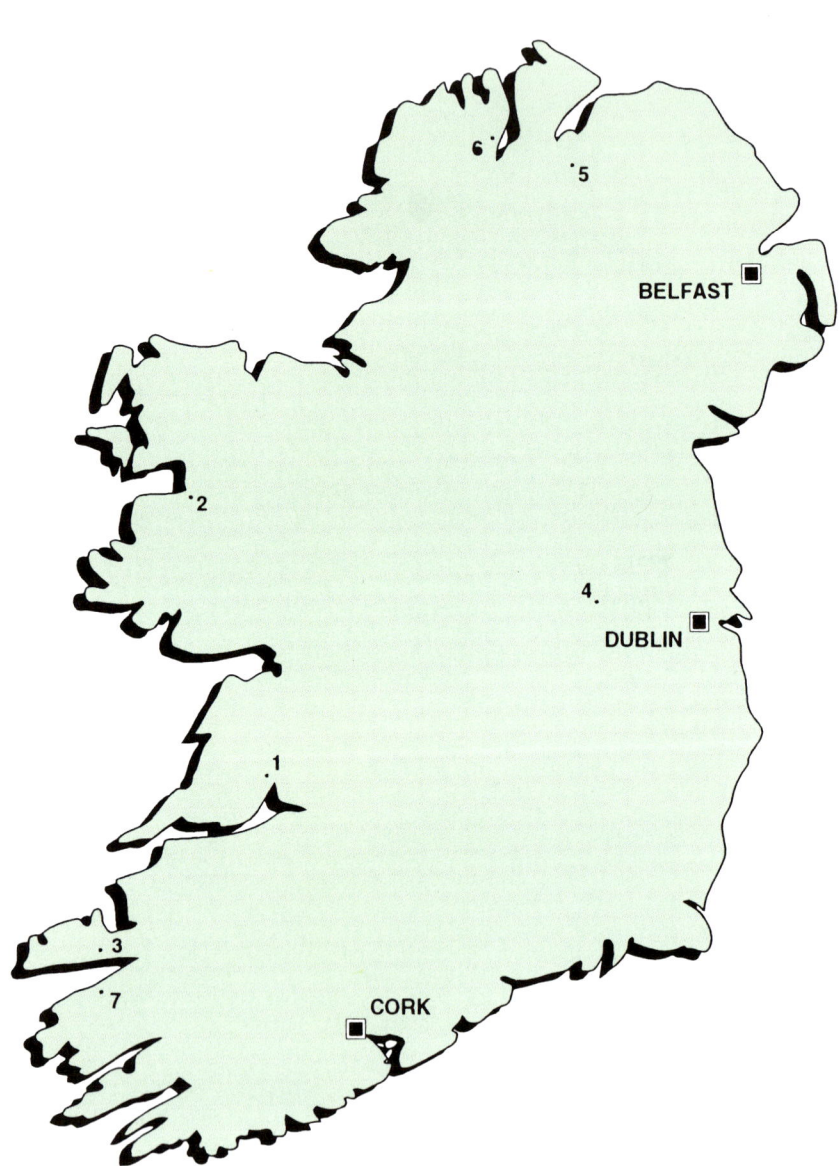

ESTABLISHMENTS IN IRELAND

Map ref.		Page no.
1	Claureen Health Farm	226
2	Cloona Health Centre	228
3	Lios Dana	230
4	Old Glebe	232
5	Raspberry Hill Health Farm	234
6	Rathmullan House	236
7	Signal Box Health Farm	238

| IRELAND | **CLAUREEN HEALTH FARM
COUNTY CLARE** |

Claureen Health Farm
Ennis   Co Clare   Ireland
☏   010 353 65 28969

Price category E∗

This busy little health farm is now into its ninth year, and specialises in slimming, fitness, beauty and relaxation.

The actual premises are on the site of an 80 acre farm, adjacent to Ennis town in the county of Clare, not far from the majestic cliffs of Moher, made famous in the epic film *Ryan's Daughter*.

The general aim is to help guests improve their general state of health in a relaxed and holiday-like atmosphere.

The programme is planned for a stay of at least a week, with guests arriving on Sunday evening and departing the following Saturday afternoon.

On arrival, all guests have an initial consultation with a member of staff to discuss personal requirements for the week. Most treatments take place in the morning - with afternoons left free for walks through the lovely countryside, trips to the coast or other scenic areas (transport by Claureen's own mini-bus at no extra cost), and any other activities in the area such as swimming or horse-riding.

The menus are wholesome and nutritious, designed to encourage weight loss.

Accommodation is mainly in twin-bedded rooms with shared bathroom facilities, although single accommodation is available on request - only one room has an en suite bathroom.

Treatments & Activities
One body massage is included in the tariff which also includes aerobics classes and supervised exercising in the gym, squash, spa baths, sauna, Slendertone and sunbed.

Extra beauty treatments such as facials IR£14 and hairdressing can be arranged.

Tariff
Inclusive weekly tariff IR£155 per person in shared double/twin room or IR£175 in single room.

Travel Directions
From the town of Ennis take the N85 road to Lahinch for approximately a mile. The Claureen Health Farm is on the left hand side of the road.

Nearest railway station Limerick approximately 24 miles.

IRELAND

CLOONA
COUNTY MAYO

Cloona Health Centre
Westport   Co Mayo   Ireland
☏   010 353 98 25251

| 10 | ☆ 🍃 ♨ ☯ ✴ ✖ 🍇 |

Price category E✻

Formerly an old Irish mill, Cloona was restored in 1973 and is Ireland's longest established residential health centre.

Situated three miles from Westport, County Mayo, and just a mile from the coast, Cloona boasts panoramic views over Clew Bay and its islands. It is an idyllic spot to relax and regenerate. There is free time during the week to explore the beautiful countryside and bikes are provided.

The programme has been designed to help achieve a higher standard of physical and mental well-being through cleansing, exercise and relaxation, and runs from Sunday to Saturday, February to November. It is primarily a cleansing course with a strong emphasis on relaxation and exercise, and therefore actual weight loss is not the most important consideration.

This is a strictly no smoking/no alcohol establishment, with no ordinary tea or coffee available, only herbal teas to which guests are invited to help themselves. A special diet using the principles of food combining aims to give the digestive system a rest, while helping eliminate toxins.

All visitors receive a short massage in the evening after taking a sauna, to help the cleansing process and stimulate circulation. Brisk daily walks are an integral part of the weekly programme, and provide an opportunity to enjoy the outstanding scenery surrounding Cloona. Talks on nutrition and herbal remedies in the home are also included in the week's programme. Prospective guests are advised to wean themselves off tea, coffee and sugar during the week prior to their visit, and to avoid heavy meals on the days leading up to the course.

A week at Cloona is designed to be a complete break from the stresses of modern life - there is no television and use of radios is not encouraged - guests are expected to fully participate in the week's course.

Be prepared to enjoy the rugged beauty of Ireland's west coast, and pack essentials such as walking shoes and rain wear, along with track suit and swimsuit.

Treatments

Daily treatments included in the overall weekly charge include yoga class, brisk organised daily walk, sauna and twenty minute massage.

Optional therapeutic full body massage or reflexology treatment IR£12 each.

Tariff

Price of a week's course which includes accommodation for six nights, all meals, treatments, classes and talks is IR£198 for a single room and IR£363 for two persons sharing a double/twin-bedded room.

Fees are payable at the commencement of the course, and a booking deposit of IR£50 per person is required.

Travel Directions

Cloona is 1 mile from the main Louisburgh Road in Westport, County Mayo. It is within driving distance of both Knock and Galway airports.

Nearest railway station Westport 3 miles.

IRELAND

LIOS DANA
COUNTY KERRY

Lios Dana Natural Living Centre
Inch-Annascaul   Co Kerry   Ireland
☎ 010 353 66 58189

Price category E✽

If you long to get away from it all completely, spending time recovering vitality and energy with others of the same mind, then Lios Dana Natural Living Centre is for you.

Anne Hyland and Michael Travers acquired the Centre in 1985 and renovated it for residential courses and retreat holidays.

It is essentially a holistic retreat, located on the side of a hill with magnificent views of the Dingle Peninsula, the beautiful Inch Strand and the Atlantic Ocean. Here you can take a walk along four miles of deserted sandy beaches and dunes, and watch (or even swim alongside!) dolphins frolicking in an ocean warmed by the Gulf Stream. There are many wonderful sights to be seen - the views of the mountains around

Dingle are forever changing with the light and atmosphere of the mild Kerry climate.

The ambience is inspirational and supportive, promoting vitality and recovery of energy. Stays can be restful or active, with good food, clean air, interesting company and participation in activities such as yoga, meditation, cooking, art, aidido, shiatsu-acupressure, walking, swimming, fishing, birdwatching, seaweed gathering, etc.

The Centre is purpose built - with eight guest bedrooms all with wash-hand basins, a large recreation room, library/drawing room, dining room and kitchen.

Macrobiotic, vegetarian and seafood meals are prepared at the Centre, the aim being to provide balanced nutrition by choosing varied ingredients for individual needs. The food is wholesome Irish cooking at its best with home-made breads, jams, soups, spreads, fresh fruit and organic vegetables.

Discussion of diet, nutrition and natural health care may be included in weekend or weekly programmes when requested.

No beauty treatments are available, just lots of healthy outdoor activities and excursions.

Tariff

Rates include accommodation, activities and meals.

The weekend rate per person for a two night stay is IR£60, and for a weekly stay (six nights) IR£185 per person.

Travel Directions

From Cork (2 hours drive) take N22 to Castlemaine and then R561 to Inch. From Dublin (5 hours drive) use N7, N21 and R561 to Inch. Kerry airport is 20 miles away (direct flights from Luton and Heathrow).

Nearest railway station Tralee 18 miles.

IRELAND

OLD GLEBE
COUNTY WESTMEATH

The Old Glebe Health Farm
Kinnegad Killucan Co Westmeath Ireland
☏ 010 353 44 74263   Fx 010 353 44 74429

Price category C✶

Just an hour's drive from Dublin is the peaceful health spa of Old Glebe, owned and managed by Sarah Pringle.

Set amid mature parkland in Westmeath countryside, Old Glebe is the first health farm in Ireland to introduce a medically-supervised health programme.

On arrival guests are offered a brief but thorough health consultation, including medical history, weight and blood pressure checks by the Old Glebe's doctor. Individual requirements are then discussed and arranged.

This is a small and friendly health farm with good facilities. All the bedrooms have en suite bathroom, and there is a cosy open fire in the lounge.

The daily rate includes a G5 massage and choice of heat treatment - sauna, jacuzzi or steam bath, as well as unlimited use of gym equipment, heated indoor pool, exercise classes, tennis and squash courts.

The Old Glebe prides itself on its delicious Irish cuisine, with organic fruit and vegetables from its own gardens, and lean steaks, poultry and eggs from its own farm.

Breakfast is taken in your bedroom and calorie controlled diets are available for slimmers. Guests wishing to fast for a couple of days are also catered for and given encouragement.

Treatments

Many optional hair, body, beauty and alternative health treatments can be reserved at Old Glebe. These include a full medical screen from IR£60; osteopathy IR£25 per session; stress management programme IR£35; physiotherapy IR£15 per session; facials from IR£10; aromatherapy IR£20; algae bath and body wrap IR£16; Slendertone IR£8 or 4 sessions for IR£28; course of 5 sunbed treatments IR£20; waxing from IR£3.

Treatment prices DO NOT include VAT.

Tariff

To achieve optimum benefit, a five night stay is recommended from Sunday evening until after lunch on Friday.

Single room with en suite bathroom IR£75 per night or IR£375 for five nights.

Sharing double room with en suite bathroom IR£60/IR£65 per person per night or IR£300/IR£325 for five nights.

Please note these rates DO NOT include VAT which is added to accounts at the current rate.

Two night weekend rates from Friday evening to Sunday afternoon are IR£150 per person - this rate includes VAT.

Travel Directions

From Dublin take N4 west for 40 miles. After reaching Kinnegad turn onto Killucan road for 4 miles. Old Glebe is on the left, at the stop sign in the village.

Nearest railway station Mullingar 8 1/2 miles.

RASPBERRY HILL HEALTH FARM
COUNTY LONDONDERRY

The Raspberry Hill Health Farm
29 Bonds Glen Road Londonderry Northern Ireland BT47 3ST
✆ 0504 398259 & 398000

6

Price category E✻

The Raspberry Hill Health Farm is situated in the scenic Bond's Glen in the picturesque foothills of the Sperrin Mountains in Northern Ireland. It takes its unusual name from the wild fruit growing in profusion in this lovely area on the County Tyrone/Derry borders of Northern Ireland.

The health farm is the residential expansion of a highly successful weight reducing clinic established over ten years ago, and is personally supervised and managed by Claire and Alfie Danton. The farm caters mainly for the visitor wanting to lose weight and re-educate eating habits and attitudes to food. However, many guests come to enjoy a peaceful, stress-free break in delightful rural surroundings.

All accommodation is in tastefully decorated single, double and twin-bedded rooms with en suite shower and toilet. There are also some three and four bedded rooms available with en suite facilities.

The day's routine is very relaxed and informal - starting with fruit juice and a multivitamin tablet at 9.00am and some optional exercise such as brisk walking. A light but adequate breakfast is then taken, followed by the treatments and classes of the day, with a break for a healthy, low calorie lunch. Dinner consists of a hearty salad with fish or lean meat, and a low calorie dessert such as yoghurt, with fruit, tea or coffee. A drink and fruit are served before bedtime.

In the evenings there are aerobic classes and other amenities to pass the time or the beautiful surrounding area can be explored. Slimmers should resist the quaint local pubs in nearby Donemana, which also has late night shopping most evenings. Less active guests can relax and watch television in either of Raspberry Hill's two main lounges.

Treatments & Activities

A week's stay includes daily counselling at weight reducing clinic, Slendertone treatment, sauna, steam cabinets, hydro-bath and full use of the gym. Sunbeds and solarium are coin-operated at £3 per session. Optional alternative health treatments can be arranged on request - full body massage £12 and reflexology £10.

Other activities available include 9-hole putting green, tennis, indoor bowls, table tennis and badminton. Bicycles may be hired free of charge to explore the many local places of interest.

Alfie Danton can occasionally be persuaded to give visitors a short flight over the area in his small plane!

Tariff

The minimum length of stay is a week (six nights), as the weight loss programme cannot be effective in a lesser period.

The weekly tariff is £150 per person sharing accommodation or £200 in a single room - from 7.00pm Sunday until midday the following Saturday.

Travel Directions

From Eglington village (1/2 mile from airport, 8 miles from city of Londonderry) turn left onto Claudy road and head for A6 (south). Continue on A6 for 4 miles turning right onto B74 - Bond's Glen Road is 1/4 mile from this point.

Nearest railway station Londonderry approximately 10 miles.

IRELAND

RATHMULLAN HOUSE
COUNTY DONEGAL

Rathmullan House
Lough Swilly   Rathmullan   Letterkenny   Co Donegal   Ireland
℡ 010 353 74 58188   Fx 010 353 74 58200

| 18 |

Price category D

This gracious early 19th century house enjoys an outstanding situation in the glorious countryside of north Donegal. Its beautiful gardens slope down to the sandy shores of Lough Swilly, with views across the lough to the Inishowen Peninsula.

Privately owned by Rob and Robin Wheeler, Rathmullan House has won many awards and praise over the years. The light filled rooms reflect the beauty of their surroundings, especially the silky drapes of the Arabian-style ceiling in the dining room, and the public rooms overlooking the lake.

Log burning fireplaces, crystal chandeliers, antiques and a charming and friendly staff make for a very enjoyable stay.

One outstanding attraction to guests seeking a healthy holiday are the Egyptian Baths, which opened in 1989 and house a heated indoor ionised salt water pool 40' long, sauna and steam room with separate changing areas.

Private sessions in the steam room or sauna are charged at IR£1.50 per hour, and during the summer swimming lessons can be arranged. Tennis courts are also available.

Treatments

No beauty treatments given, but qualified masseuse and reflexologist Caitlin Gallagher gives a variety of therapeutic body treatments. Head and face massage IR£7.50; back massage IR12.50; head, face and back massage IR£15; whole body massage lasting 1 1/4 hours IR£35. Reflexology treatments are an hour long and more than one treatment is required for a healing response.

Tariff

Rathmullan House offers the following accommodation and rates for stays of a minimum of three nights. Prices are per person and include VAT but NOT service charge:

Master suite with views, en suite bathroom and sitting area IR£47.50 bed/breakfast or IR£60 half board;

Master bedroom with en suite bathroom and sitting area IR£40 bed/breakfast or IR£54 half board;

Standard room with bathroom IR£32.50 bed/breakfast or IR£47 half board;

Family room (large garret rooms with bathroom) IR£27.50 bed/breakfast or IR£42 half board;

Budget room without bathroom IR£22.50 bed/breakfast or IR£38 half board.

Children sharing with parents 50% discount. Special weekend or two night half board rates cost from IR£88 to IR£128 per person.

All tariffs include use of the Egyptian Baths and tennis courts.

Travel Directions

From Letterkenny take the R245 road to Rathmelton, then follow the signs and the R247 road to Rathmullan.

No railways in Donegal - various express bus services to Letterkenny approximately 5 miles from Rathmullan House.

| IRELAND | THE SIGNAL BOX
COUNTY KERRY |

The Signal Box Health Farm
Glenbeigh   Co Kerry   Ireland
☏   010 353 66 68240   (Fx)   010 353 66 68431

Price category D✲

A health farm with a difference is to be found at the Signal Box in Co. Kerry. Sited in a little village at the foot of the Seefin mountain, close to a wonderful four mile sweep of clean sands with excellent bathing, it offers a range of health cures and diets to suit everyone.

The health farm has a large garden and is sited in Glenbeigh's former railway station, just 300 yards from the famous Ring of Kerry. It has been lovingly modernised by its German owners Johanna von Johnston-Lopau and Helmuth Lopau with spacious lounge and comfortable dining room both with cosy open fires.

Some rooms have en suite showers and toilet facilities and others wash-basin, two rooms have open fires and all have television.

The Signal Box is the only health farm in Great Britain and Ireland to offer the Schroth (Dry Diet) metabolism cure.

In Germany, the 'Schroth Kur' has been running successfully for 150 years in over 2,000 centres and it is also practised in Austria, Switzerland, Canada and the USA.

Treatments

The Signal Box offers no beauty treatments, specialising only in two continental natural health 'cures'.

The Schroth treatment comprises packs, dieting and a system of alternating 'dry' and 'drinking' days, resulting in the detoxification of the whole body which is relieved of excess water and fat. The whole process is carried out under medical supervision (one examination per week), and is reputed to be especially helpful in cases of fluid retention, rheumatoid arthritis, catarrh and chronic skin conditions.

A period of three weeks is recommended for this 'cure', although a modified version based on the same principles is available for guests with only a week to spare.

Because of the nature of the treatment, no more than six guests are accommodated at any one time, and when taking the 'cure' guests do not share rooms.

Kneipp Hydro-treatments have been introduced as an alternative to the Schroth Kur - these also last a week and involve water applications to deal with a variety of conditions.

Tariff

All treatments start on Sunday and finish on Saturday.

Prices cover accommodation, 'cure' diet, exercises, special treatments, massage, yoga lessons and/or Callanetics.

Weekly tariff for both types of treatment is IR£220 in standard room or IR£270 in spacious room with en suite facilities

Medical fees for examinations cost IR£12 initially and IR£10 subsequently.

Healthy weekend breaks have recently been introduced at the Signal Box - these do not include either of the continental treatments and the inclusive cost is IR£96 for a single room with en suite facilities or IR£80 per person sharing. A single room without facilities costs IR£80 for the weekend.

Travel Directions

Glenbeigh is in the far south west of Ireland, on the N70 approximately 16 miles from Kerry.

Nearest railway station Killarney approximately 16 miles.

(Collection from Farranfore airport or Killarney railway station can be arranged.)

BRITISH SPAS
A SPLASHING REVIVAL?

The Roman Bath, Bath, Avon

The plugged up waters of British spas may soon be flowing again! Ambitious plans have been drawn up to develop the untapped potential of some of our most attractive spa towns - to turn the spa waters back on for tasting and bathing and to provide exciting 21st century health hydros offering the latest health and beauty treatments.

The 1990s mark our integration into a continent rich in therapeutic and thermal springs. Europeans of all ages visit their spas regularly, enjoying the simple pleasures of bathing in beautifully warm curative waters and receiving health restorative treatments. In France, Germany and Switzerland, spa use is positively encouraged by governments, trade unions and the medical profession, with most health insurance schemes providing cover for the cost of treatments. Balneotherapy (treatment with spa water) offers a safe, enjoyable and effective alternative to drug therapy, especially for those with problems of mobility, such as elderly people and those recovering from accidents or surgery.

European spas have prospered, becoming vibrant resorts and attracting visitors all year round. Beautiful surroundings, pleasant shopping areas and an abundance of flowers and gardens create a pleasantly relaxed environment. Visitors are welcomed with affordable spa treatment centres available to everyone, and a bed for every budget - in comfortable hotels or well-run campsites equipped with modern conveniences. Good sporting facilities and a busy cultural calendar including music and flower festivals are other tourist attractions.

In parts of Europe, assiduous use is made of hot thermal spring water, helping conserve energy. It is tapped to heat schools, hospitals and domestic water supplies and used to wash the streets and melt away the snow. Unfortunately in Britain, we do not make such resourceful use of this natural asset and the hot springs run away wasted and unused.

British spas originated in pre-Roman times, developing from mineral springs in holy wells. 'Taking the waters' was a standard medical practice in Tudor times, and continued into the hey day of the spa, the late Georgian and Victorian eras. Established resorts like Bath, Leamington Spa and Harrogate became part of the social calendar for royalty and rich society, seeking relief from problems caused by the excesses of their over-indulgent lifestyles. Huge hotels and health hydros were built to accommodate these rich visitors in style, together with bath houses and pump rooms designed on classical Roman lines.

The advent of the railways brought many more visitors flocking to the spas, creating wealth and prosperity for these attractive inland resorts. The boom lasted until the onset of the First World War, when the spas' popularity began to wane. The creation of the National Health Service in 1948 caused further serious decline.

As the new pharmaceutical industry grew rapidly, so the British medical profession chose to treat patients with drugs promising instantaneous results rather than the gentler, more gradual cures afforded by spa treatments. Slowly, NHS use of the spas was phased out and today, the only spa water still used therapeutically is Buxton's, in the town's Royal Devonshire Hospital.

Continental spas fared better, becoming medically orientated with attractive new hydrotherapy facilities and modern treatment clinics. European doctors continued prescribing traditional spa treatments, but now had the option of combining them with effective drug therapy, giving patients the best of both types of care.

Another important reason for the success of continental spas is that European health insurance (the equvalent of schemes like BUPA) is taken out by most of the population, and covers the cost of spa treatments like fango, hydotherapy and thalassotherapy, when medically prescribed.

The pharmaceutical industry sounded the death knell for the British spa; how ironic that today our search for natural remedies rckindles interest in one of our oldest assets. As the saying goes - the wheel has turned full circle.

SPA WATER PROPERTIES
There are three main categories of spa water, some spas having more than one type of spring:

1) *Chalybeate water* contains iron salts including ferrous sulphite, and is taken medicinally for blood disorders such as anaemia. Royal Tunbridge Wells and Trefriw Wells have chalybeate spring water rich in minerals especially iron.
The water has no smell but tastes metallic.

2) *Sulphur waters* (containing hydrogen sulphur) are immediately recognised by their 'bad egg' smell - they taste equally foul, but are said to 'purify' the blood if consumed, and to treat skin disorders when bathing.
Harrogate, Llandridnod Wells and Strathpeffer have sulphur water, as do many continental spas, where effective filtration removes the unpleasant smell.

3) *Saline water* is known for its purgative properties, and contains various dissolved salts. Although it can be taken internally as a purifier and laxative, its most therapeutic use is for bathing. Bath, Leamington Spa and Droitwich have saline water. The Droitwich brine contains 30 per cent natural salts, and like the Dead Sea is ten times more concentrated than normal sea water. The huge measure of two and a half pounds of salt to each gallon of water gives the water its incredible buoyancy, unique in all Europe.

THE BRITISH SPA FEDERATION
177 Windermere Way   Stourport-on-Severn
Hereford & Worcester   DY13 8QE
℃   0386 565000

This small organisation of 13 spa members was founded in 1975 to promote, revive and develop public awareness of British spas. The Federation has recently become a limited company, and is based near Droitwich, where the highly successful brine baths complex is Britain's first major spa development this century.

The Federation recently launched Spa 2000, an initiative to actively regenerate interest in British spas and get the waters back on for tasting and bathing. It is looking for ways to interest investors in developing spas on highly successful continental lines, incorporating health farm and beauty treatments as well as treatment therapies.

The Federation is also organising medical seminars, to interest doctors in the concept of spas and the value of restorative treatments.

The following spas are members of the British Spas Federation:-

BATH

Tourist Information Centre
The Colonnades   11-13 Bath Street   Avon   BA1 1SW
☏ 0225 462831

Bath's hot spa waters have bubbled out of the limestone at 40°C for centuries. A toxic bacterial organism closed down the last of the treatment facilities in 1978, and although this has now been eliminated, the spa bathing facilities remain closed. Visitors can sip a tepid glass of metallic-tasting spring water in the elegant Pump Room.

Ambitious plans to redevelop the bathing facilities in 1990 were halted when the contracted company went into liquidation. However Bath council are now considering other schemes, which in the course of time will hopefully result in Bath's re-emergence as a leading European spa.

The hot thermal water is ideal for bathing, and useful for treating rheumatism, arthritis, high blood pressure and metabolic diseases.

BUXTON

Tourist Information Centre
The Crescent   Derbyshire   SK17 6BQ
☏ 0298 27639

Buxton's pale blue thermal waters lie in a subterranean reservoir for 20 years before coming up to the surface at a temperature of 28°C.

Water can be sampled at the drinking fountain next to the Pump Room in the town centre.

Thermal water is used for orthopaedic treatments at the Devonshire Royal Hospital, and in the Buxton spa swimming pool.

Water is excellent for bottling and bathing, and benefits rheumatic and arthritic disorders.

CHELTENHAM SPA

Tourist Information Centre
77 Promenade   Gloucestershire   GL50 1PP
☏ 0242 522878

No bathing facilities here, but Britain's only alkaline spring water is available for drinking.

There are currently no plans to reopen bathing facilities.

Water said to benefit circulation and digestive disorders and anaemia.

DROITWICH

Tourist Information Centre
St Richard's House Victoria Square Hereford & Worcester WR9 8DS
✆ 0905 774312

This is the British Spas Federation greatest achievement to date!

After overcoming some local opposition, the old brine baths were demolished and a new complex designed on modern lines opened in 1985.

Droitwich Brine Baths are owned and managed by Compass Healthcare, who operate the adjoining private hospital and specialist knee clinic.

In 1990 over 150,000 visitors used the baths, and to cope with the demand a second brine pool is planned which will also offer continental spa treatments like fango.

The brine baths are kept free in the mornings for various hydrotherapy treatments carried out by physiotherapists on patients recovering from such diverse health problems as strokes, arthritis and major orthopaedic surgery.

After midday, the public can enjoy the spa (no more than 20 people at any one time), together with other reasonably priced facilities in the complex - sauna, massage, beauty treatments and fitness assessments.

The very salty water is marvellous for bathing and hydrotherapy because of its buoyancy. Even non-swimmers can relax floating in these unique waters, kept at a constant temperature of 33°C. Cost of a session is a very reasonable £5 or £9 per couple, and includes sauna, brine bath, use of towels and bathrobe and refreshments.

The water is not suitable for drinking, of course, but because of its buoyancy is an ideal medium for hydrotherapy.

HARROGATE

Tourist Information Centre
Royal Baths Assembly Rooms Crescent Road North Yorkshire HG1 2RR
✆ 0423 525666

The cold sulphur water tastes rotten and smells of bad eggs! This does not deter the determined spa seeker from sampling it in the Royal Pump Room Museum in the town center.

Although the bathing facilities closed in 1969, the magnificent Turkish baths have recently been fully restored and are now open seven days a week, with separate sessions for men and women. A session lasting two hours costs £5.50.

Harrogate will be re-established as a leading spa centre in the very near future, when an exciting development centred on the Old Swan Hotel is completed. Millions are being spent upgrading the hotel and building an adjacent continental spa complex. Work should be completed in 1993 and includes two indoor pools using spa water for treatments, sauna, solarium, Turkish baths, plunge pools, hot rooms, hot tub, water massage, hydrotherapy, algae baths, mud and fango pack treatments. Medical consultations will be available, as well as indoor exercise facilities - exercise studio, gymnasium, fitness assessments.

Harrogate's spa water is used to treat rheumatic, digestive and skin troubles.

LEAMINGTON SPA

Tourist Information Centre
Jephson Lodge Jephson Gardens The Parade Warwickshire CV32 4AB
✆ 0926 311470

The mildly laxative spa water can be sampled in the fountain of the Pump Room cafe, and tastes unpleasantly of salt and iron.

Unfortunately treatment facilities at the Spa Pump Rooms finished at the end of 1990 - until then 60,000 patients a year, mainly NHS referrals, were treated by an outstanding hydro/physiotherapy department.

Over £1 million was needed to modernise the old building which was in a bad state of repair, and tenders were invited by the Council. A private investor's scheme to demolish and replace sections of the historic building, installing a modern health spa with the latest treatments and beauty therapies seemed an ideal opportunity to put Leamington back on the map as a spa.

Unfortunately a few locals opposed the idea so strongly that the project was delayed and finally cancelled. The old facility was closed down, and highly specialised spa physiotherapists made redundant.

Leamington Spa's water is saline and excellent for hydrotherapy.

LLANDRINDOD WELLS

Tourist Information Centre
Town Hall Powys LD1 6AA
✆ 0597 822600

This beautiful little spa town has a heritage of Victorian and Edwardian architecture. The Pump Room offers three types of spring water to sample by the glass - sulphur, saline and magnesium. Visitors to the Pump Room can also try the popular beauty treatments using the magnesium spring water with French mud, introduced in 1990.

No bathing facilities at present, but future developments likely.
Water used to treat skin disorders.

MALVERN

Tourist Information Centre
Winter Gardens Complex Grange Road Hereford & Worcester WR14 3HB
🕿 0684 892289

Malvern's spa water flows from springs in the Malvern Hills.

The water, famous for its purity, is successfully bottled by Schweppes and exported all over the world.

Visitors can sample the water from St Anne's Well and the Holy Well situated outside the town.

Currently no treatment or bathing facilities are available, but possibility of the Old Tudor Hotel (now fully modernised) opening up a former spa area in the basement as a treatment and leisure centre, utilising Malvern water.

Water is exceptionally pure and makes ideal drinking water.

MATLOCK BATH

Tourist Information Centre
The Pavilion Derbyshire DE4 3NR
🕿 0629 55082

Known as "Little Switzerland" because of its rugged scenery and spectacular cable car ride, Matlock Bath is a charming town whose spa water can be sampled at the Victorian pump in the tourist information centre.

No hydrotherapy or spa bathing facilities in the town yet, but the thermal water which emerges from the spring at a constant 20°C can be enjoyed in the swimming pools of the New Bath Hotel and in the children's paddling pool in the park.

Three acres of land alongside the river has been proposed as a site for future spa development with a new hydro facility.

In 1990, Albert Rockach's Deepwood Mining company was drilling for minerals in the hills outside the town and struck a major new source of pure mineral water. The enterprising Mr Rockach immediately set up a profitable bottling plant at the new source.

Even more exciting is the company's discovery of a major new thermal spring within the underground caves, opening up the possibility of a major spa development of enormous commercial potential.

County planners have already given the go-ahead for a £100 million scheme to build a health and leisure facility, with hotels, restaurants and car parks. Extensive spa treatments would be available using hot and cold spa waters, sulphur water, and turquoise volcanic muds for bathing and skin treatments.

Treatment and bathing facilities would be located in the underground caverns and grottoes, with internal lifts connecting directly to the hotels above.

The whole project will take a number of years to build, but is already being seen as one of the most exciting spa developments this century.

TREFRIW WELLS

Trefriw Gwynedd LL27 OJS
℅   0492 640057

Trefriw Wells is the newest member of the British Spa Federation, and unlike the other spas is not a resort as such, just a mineral rich spring bubbling from a Welsh mountainside cleft.

Originally created by the Romans, the magnificent Cyclopean Bath House built in 1743 is still intact and contains a huge Welsh slate bath and artefacts of times gone by. The Victorian Pump Room and Bath House is now a tea room, gift shop and museum.

Trefriw Wells was saved from demolition by owner Tony Rowlands, who now bottles and sells the iron rich water using a highly sophisticated filter. It has passed stringent tests to become a licensed medicine in Germany.

The water is particularly valuable to those with iron deficiencies who cannot tolerate pharmaceutical preparations.

There are plans to develop bathing facilities at Trefriw Wells in the next few years.

TUNBRIDGE WELLS

Tourist Information Centre
Monson House   Monson Way   Kent   TN1 1LQ
℅   0892 515675

Tunbridge Wells is another chalybeate (iron rich) spring.

Visitors can sample the icy cold water served by 'the dipper' on summer afternoons from the spring inside the entrance to the Pantiles (the colonnaded tree-lined shopping area).

The iron water is taken medicinally for blood disorders.

No spa bathing facilities are planned at the moment.

STRATHPEFFER

Tourist Information Centre
The Square   Ross-shire   IV14 9DW
✆   0997 21415

The UK's most northerly spa 20 miles from Inverness has had a new pavilion built for visitors wanting to sample the sulphur and iron waters. The Victorian station has also been tastefully restored.

There are no bathing facilities, but possibly an exciting future development as a spa and ski resort using the castle and a cable railway into the unused snowfields of Ben Wyvis.

WOODHALL SPA

Tourist Information Centre
The Cottage Museum   Iddlesleigh Road   Lincolnshire   LN10 6SH
✆   0526 53775

A spa in name only! Although a member of the British Spas Federation, Woodhall Spa no longer uses spa water, mud treatments or hydrotherapy. Sadly the source became contaminated some years ago, and a new pure source has yet to be laid on.

It is, however, a peaceful and attractive Lincolnshire town set amid pine and birch woods just 20 miles from Lincoln.

Droitwich Brine Pool

A GLOSSARY OF TREATMENTS & THERAPIES

ACUPRESSURE

A gentle finger pressure applied to the meridian points of the body - these are the channels of magnetic energy connecting the organs of the body. A long treatment taking at least 1 1/2 hours.

ACUPUNCTURE

An ancient form of Chinese medicine, again using the meridians of the body to regulate the life energy (Chi). Very fine needles are painlessly inserted to restore function and relieve pain, imparting a relaxed and invigorating effect.

Other types of acupuncture are sometimes offered without use of needles. Instead these use electro and laser treatments.

AROMATHERAPY

A pressure point massage using essential oils with various therapeutic properties specifically chosen for each individual after an initial consultation.

BIO-PEEL

Special facial devised by René Guinot which removes the dead skin cells and leaves the face smoother with a clearer complexion. Gives a real boost to the skin's appearance.

BLITZ JET DOUCHE

A treatment used in continental spas and now becoming popular in the UK. The recipient stands in a tiled area and is massaged from a distance of about 12 feet by a powerful jet of warmed water from a hose. The therapist massages the entire body from feet upwards using this hose - finishing with an optional cold water spray.

Quite breathtaking!

BODY SCRUB

A treatment recommended on its own or as a preparation for other body treatments or tanning. Dead skin cells are removed and the exfoliation cleanses and invigorates the body.

BODY WRAP / HERBAL WRAP / SEAWEED WRAP

Wonderfully relaxing treatment in which the body is covered in various oils and gels and then wrapped in a sheet steamed in aromatic herbs. As the recipient lies gently perspiring, toxins and excess fluid are eliminated from the body.

BUST TREATMENT

An exfoliation treatment is followed by the application of specialised products and massage, designed to tone, firm and strengthen the skin, helping improve bust shape.

CELLU M6

A new electrical driven massage treatment which folds and sucks the skin between two motorised rollers, aiding lymph flow and circulation. It has interchangeable heads and can be used on many parts of the body including the head. Cellu M6 is usually offered as either a stress relief or detoxification treatment.

CATHIODERMIE

Another treatment from René Guinot, which uses a mild electrical current to effect a deep cleanse of the skin. This oxygenates the outer skin layer, improving its texture and encouraging regeneration. The treatment, which can be used on other parts of the body as well as the face, includes a mask and lasts about 1 1/2 hours.

As this is such a thorough cleanse, the skin must be allowed time to recover. Sun-bathing and make-up should be avoided on the same day.

COLONIC IRRIGATION

Washing out of the bowel by means of a gentle enema. Presently only available at Shrubland Hall and Bournemouth Centre of Complementary Medicine. Thorneyholme Hall plan to make it an optional alternative health treatment in the near future.

ELECTROLYSIS

A method of removing unwanted hair permanently, using an electrically charged needle to the hair root. Can be expensive as each hair has to be removed separately. Especially good for removal of facial hair.

FACIAL

The most popular treatment in the beauty salon. The face and neck is thoroughly cleansed, toned and moisturised using products suited to individual skin conditions. There are many types of different facials, some with strangely undescriptive names like Paris and Hollywood. Beauty therapists can explain the differences and advise.

FANGO THERAPY

Application of mineralised mud, mixed with spa water to the consistency of plasticine, heated and used as a poultice to cover joints or areas of the body affected with arthritis or related conditions. The pack retains the heat for at least 30 minutes.

FARADIC EXERCISE

Passive electrically controlled exercise to tone and firm the body, through pads strapped to the muscles causing a tickling or tingling sensation depending on the faradic current used. Slendertone is the most well known type of faradic treatment and several sessions are necessary to effect an improvement.

FLOATARIUM / FLOAT ROOM / FLOATATION TANK

A covered bath or shallow pool containing a saturated solution of Epsom salts in water allowing the body to float effortlessly. After immersion, the lights are turned down until total darkness results. Stress and fatigue are relieved by the profound level of relaxation possible, with no awareness of gravity, temperature, light or sound. An amazing experience.

G5 MASSAGE

A deep gyratory massage using various electrically driven applicator heads (five originally, hence the name G5) on different parts of the body. The treatment relieves tiredness and tension and helps tone the body. Gives a much stronger massage than is possible using the hands alone.

GALVANIC TREATMENTS

Often used in conjuction with faradic treatments. Galvanic current encourages the absorption of liquids into the skin, by using current-conducting clay and electrodes on parts of the body needing firming, as in Ionithermie treatments.

HOMOEOPATHY

A form of alternative medicine which boosts the body's healing ability by using highly diluted and specially prepared forms of plant, mineral and animal substances. The remedies are prepared taking into account the personality as well as the symptoms of the individual.

HYDROTHERAPY

Therapeutic treatment involving the use of water in its application. Helps to cleanse the pores, improve the circulation and exercise the muscles. Heated thermal baths are used extensively in spas along with modified exercise to aid arthritis and mobility.

IONITHERMIE

A range of facial and slimming treatments for correction of cellulite and improvement of skin and muscle tone. The treatment uses gentle galvanic stimuli with thermal clay and biologically active natural ingredients. The strength of the stimuli can be varied according to need and tolerance! Can result in immediate inch loss.

INFRA-RED

Treatment uses healing infra-red light to treat painful muscles and other parts of the body. The lamps are placed over the affected area helping muscles relax and increasing the circulation of the blood.

IRIDOLOGY

A form of complementary medicine which uses the study of the iris as a form of diagnosis. Iridology claims to reveal genetic weaknesses and tendencies in the body which may be causing health problems. Lifestyle and diet changes can then be made to help overcome these.

KARWENDEL

A continental treatment using fossil oils to relax and refresh the body. The thick tarry substance is rich in nutrients and added to a warm, therapeutic bath, stimulating the circulation and helping to clear up problem skin. Beneficial to sufferers of psoriasis and other skin conditions.

KNEIPP THERAPY

A cold water treatment used extensively in Europe but less frequently in the UK. It works through the reaction of the body to being stimulated by the cold, and improves blood supply, metabolism and helps strengthen the nervous system. Treatment consists of herbal baths or body packs (see Signal Box Health Farm entry for full description). Not as barbaric as it sounds as all procedures are carefully monitored at every stage, and the treatment is only given to a warm body in a well heated room.

MASSAGE

The most popular and available treatment in all health farms and beauty salons. Swedish body massage is the type most generally given, and uses long sweeping movements interspersed with kneading and pummelling. Fatigue and tension, but NOT, unfortunately fat, are rubbed away with the help of scented oils to reduce friction.

Very relaxing and especially beneficial to the neck and shoulder areas.

NEEDLE SHOWERS

An overhead shower with additional water outlets placed at different body levels to give a horizontal spray massage.

Pleasantly invigorating.

MOOR PEAT BATH

A hot or warm bath lasting about 20 minutes, to which a mixture of liquid peat has been added. The treatment finishes with a lie down in a warm room. Good for rheumatism sufferers.

OSTEOPATHY

The manipulation of the spine to relieve back pain, sciatica, neck and shoulder pains and various other conditions of the body.

PARAFFIN WAX BATHS

Not a bath for immersion! A thick layer of warm wax is brushed over the body which is then wrapped up to keep warm. As the body perspires, the heat draws out toxins, cleansing the pores and softening the skin.

PARAFFIN WAX FOR HANDS AND FEET

A treatment to help relieve the discomforts of arthritis, rheumatism and circulatory problems. The warmth and cleansing effects combine to leave the skin feeling soft.

PHYSIOTHERAPY

The application of various techniques including electrical muscle stimulation, remedial exercise in water and with apparatus to restore or improve the health and mobility of the body.

Especially useful in treating sports injuries.

REFLEXOLOGY

A foot massage in which pressure points in the toes and feet which correspond with other parts of the body are massaged and stimulated. Hitherto unknown health problems can sometimes be detected in this relaxing treatment.

SALT RUB

A brisk body rub given after showering. Salt is massaged all over the body by hand or with a loofah. A salt rub is often given prior to a hydrotherapy massage bath.

Very invigorating, leaves the skin soft and glowing.

SAUNA

A wooden-lined room complete with wooden benches for sitting or reclining. The room is heated with dry heat to around 40°C or more, making the body sweat profusely - a cold plunge or shower afterwards closes the pores and leaves the body glowing.

This popular heat treatment originated in Finland, and is found in virtually all health farms and health clubs.

SCOTTISH DOUCHE

A shower of alternating hot and cold water jets to stimulate the spinal column and tone up the circulation and nervous systems of the body.

SHIATSU

An oriental body therapy similar to acupressure.

The practitioner uses his/her elbows, knees, feet, palms and fingers to press along the meridian lines of the body. Shiatsu restores balance or 'oneness' by summoning energy to and from parts of the body that need it. Very therapeutic and effective in the relief of insomnia, pain and tension.

SITZ BATHS

A hip bath composed of two parts, one filled with hot water the other cold. The patient sits in the hot water with feet in the cold for a few minutes and then alternates. An effective natural treatment to improve circulation and as an aid in prostate and some gynaecological conditions.

STEAM BATH

A popular heat treatment given in its own enclosure, using steam to promote perspiration and help remove body toxins.

Like the sauna, the steam room has shelving to sit or recline on - menthol vapours can be added to the steam to aid inhalation.

STEAM CABINET

A relaxing treatment lasting about 30 minutes - unlike the steam room, the head remains outside the cabinet and is not exposed to the steam as the rest of the body gently perspires inside. Still found at many health farms.

THALASSOTHERAPY

The therapeutic use of sea-water, seaweeds and other marine components. Most popular in French spas, it is now becoming a favourite treatment in the UK too. Thalassotherapy programmes include algae baths, wraps and masks.

TURKISH BATHS

Real Turkish baths are a series of increasingly hot and humid steam rooms complete with marble slabs for reclining as the body perspires. The procedure is reversed to cool down before finishing with a tepid or cold shower and a rest. Steam rooms are sometimes incorrectly called Turkish baths. The spa town of Harrogate has a splendid example of a Turkish bath in all its glory.

UNDERWATER MASSAGE

Massage given in a warm bath by high pressure jets of water within the bath and sometimes combined with peat or seaweed. The process is helpful in breaking down cellulite and improving the circulation, but is not suitable for those with a raised blood pressure or who bruise easily.

Underwater massage can also be given by a therapist with a hand held high pressure hose.

WAXING

Removal of unwanted hair from the body and face using a warm wax thinly applied. Muslin strips are pressed onto the hairs which should be at least 1/4" long, and then removed.

Can be uncomfortable, but regrowth will be softer and take longer to show.

VITAL HARMONY

A Decleor treatment involving body exfoliation combined with aromatherapy oils to improve the elasticity of the skin. Slimming and relaxing, it leaves the body feeling smoother and firmer.

YOGA

A system of training mind and body which originated in India and is particularly helpful in the management of stress-related problems.

There are several forms of yoga, the best known one in Western countries is Hatha yoga, which uses postures and exercises emphasising the importance of breathing and relaxation.